Get Past the Tags!

How to Write

(and Read)

XML Documents

by

Jonathan Reeve Price

Copyright

Welcome to our IDEAL tutorial!

Instructions

You get step-by-step instructions on building each part of an XML document. No more abstract descriptions of syntax. You can see exactly how each tag is constructed, from beginning to end.

Diagrams

You see the structure in a large diagram, so you can tell where each piece of punctuation goes, and what the components do.

Examples

You get examples, so you can see exactly how the tags develop, and how they look when completed.

Answers

If you have questions, we have answers. Addressing the most common questions that come up in discussions, the FAQs give you context and background on the tags.

Lookup

You'll find a thorough glossary and index in the back, so you can use this book as a reference, to look up a concept, tag, or syntax.

Quick: Is this book for you?

Yes, if you are a writer.

Not a programmer. Not a suit.

Yes, if you must create content that is:

- Consistent

- Re-usable

- Modular

- Easy to send out in many formats on many platforms

- Manipulated by many programs as you write, save, and publish

No, if you are still writing with a pen.

Who am I?

I'm a writer, too. I've worked as a journalist, technical communicator, and consultant to teams of writers in more than a dozen high-tech corporations.

I got my start at Apple, creating what we called help systems, working with more than 50 other writers to create a style guide for the technical writers, as we tried to define a friendly but helpful approach to documentation.

Through workshops and online classes, I've trained more than a thousand writers in XML, content management, information architecture, and good old-fashioned task topics. My wife and I have done a lot of writing for the web, too, so we issued a book called *Hot Text: Web Writing that Works.*

The writers I've worked with have all contributed to this book. They asked questions, and I've added the answers. They showed confusion about some of the more metaphysical concepts, and I hope I have clarified these.

Most important, our conversations have shown me that XML builds on familiar ideas about writing—concepts such as structure, format, and clarity. And if we think of what we do as serving our audiences, XML helps us do that more effectively, for more people, in more formats, than ever before.

At first glance, XML looks ugly—a maze of odd punctuation and tags, with tiny bits of content tucked in between. But as we come to see the purpose behind the XML approach, we can learn how—and why—to read and write in this new way. That's why I say that the first step is: Get past the tags!

4

Contents

Overview

Why learn to read and write in XML?

To create content

To write content that medium and large organizations can publish automatically in multiple formats on multiple devices in multiple languages.

To speed up the creation of new content by reusing elements of existing material.

To make your content consistent in structure and format, across many product lines, so that many audiences can quickly find and use the information.

To understand how your content gets stored and published

To understand and work with the software that manages the content that your organization distributes.

To read and understand the tags that appear in XML and XHTML documents.

To understand the way that this approach separates what you write (your content) from its structure and its format.

To understand the way that a web browser uses three documents to build a web page—one with your content, one with a formal definition of the structure of all documents of this type, and one with a description of the formatting that must be applied to each element in your document.

To help the people who use your content

To provide users with fine-grained search results, so that they can quickly find a particular fact, not a long manual.

To help your users browse through menus and links to navigate the mass of content that you provide.

To offer content customized for important groups, such as customers, vendors, partners, reporters, financial analysts, technical folks, and even managers.

To make it possible for your systems to offer personalized content for individuals.

To manage the process

To improve the speed and efficiency of your process for creating, storing, and publishing content.

To work well with the folks who create information models describing the standard structure of each type of document that your team produces.

To work well with the designers who create templates and stylesheets that format that content.

To gather detailed feedback from your users, so you can quickly meet their changing needs.

So...What is XML, and where does it come from?

The eXtensible Markup Language (XML) is a new way of writing—and reading.

XML offers a standard way of creating a set of tags to annotate content, describing each element in the structure, so that software can format and transform the text, store its elements in a database, and publish the content in different documents on devices with many different form factors, in many languages, with constantly changing information.

That sounds a bit intimidating.

But as a writer, you may already be familiar with some of the basic tactics for clarifying our text:

- Format
- Structure
- Markup
- Language

Each of these offers a way that we can help the reader understand what we are saying. XML gives us a new version of tactics that have evolved from the earliest days of writing.

Format is the way the text looks.

Here are some examples of formatting:

> *It is easy to be heavy; hard to be light.*
> — G.K. Chesterton, *Orthodoxy*, 1909

The creative mind plays with the objects it loves.

— Carl Gustav Jung, *Psychological Types*, 1921

What's the formatting here?

- Space characters to separate one word from another
- Capital letters to indicate the start of sentences
- Capital letters to indicate the start of proper names and titles
- Punctuation to separate elements in a phrase or sentence
- New lines to separate ideas
- Fonts, sizes, indentations, line breaks, to suggest tone, attitude, relative importance

Example of lack of formatting:

```
lifeisverynicebutitlacksformitstheaimofar
ttogiveitsome—jeananouilhtherehearsal1950
```

A simple text stream (raw text) lacks all formatting, so it is difficult to distinguish one word from another, one element from another. Without formatting, we have a hard time reading, much less comprehending what we read.

Formatting provides information **about** the text.

Structure is the arrangement of the elements in the text.

Ideally, the format reveals the structure. But structure is not format.

Example of structure: A table of contents:

Introduction

Chapter 1

Chapter 2

Conclusion

Glossary

Bibliography

Index

What's the structure here?

The organization of the book's content at the highest level.

Note: This structure exists no matter what formatting gets applied.

Example of structure—An outline or menu system:

Reviewing a document

Using tracked changes

Inserting, deleting, or changing a comment

Comparing two versions of a document

Blocking a reviewer

Accepting and rejecting changes

Viewing a final version

What makes the structure here?

- The division of information into separate topics
- The hierarchical organization of the topics, and within the submenu, the sequence of topics

Structure answers questions about the relationships between elements of the text.

- What are the different elements here?
- Which element is more important than another?
- Which elements are subordinate to other elements?
- Which elements belong together?
- Which elements must be kept separate, in our mind?
- What is the sequence of elements in a particular group?

So structure provides meaningful information about the way the parts of the text play off of each other and fit together.

We need to separate our idea of format from our idea of structure.

The problem is that in a world of web pages and printed books, the formatting works to **reveal** the organization of the text. So our mind imagines that the visual expression of the underlying structure is all there is.

Antidote: Think of yourself sitting in an auditorium as a speaker comes to the podium.

Suddenly, the power fails, the computer goes dark, there is no slide deck on screen. The speaker is left without PowerPoint. Just talk.

Now, the speech has a certain organization, but because the words are in the air, invisible, you cannot SEE the structure.

The organization of the speech might be like this:

- My topic today
- Why my company is an expert on this topic
- Problems that your customers may have
- Solutions from other vendors
- Our solutions, and why they are the best
- Call to action: sign up today
- How to get in touch with me

Until the power comes back on, and the slides appear on screen, you could not see these as bullet points, that is, visibly arranged on a colorful background, in the company's favorite font, adorned with a stock photo. The formatting would make the structure **visible**. But format is not structure.

Why do I insist on this distinction?

Because in casual conversation, many people use the word "format" to mean "organization," or "standard structure." Why do they do this? I think that's because the structure of a document is so often represented, expressed, articulated in a visual way on the screen or on paper. It's hard to tell them apart.

But one of the big ideas behind XML, as you'll see, is the separation of structure from format.

One structure, many formats

Back in grade school, when we were using a big fat pencil and paper, whatever we wrote had a certain look, and that look was the only way that we were able to format the text, say, by underlining the title of our story, or writing our name in ALL CAPS.

But now that we write in a word processing application, the computer allows us to separate the text from the format. So we can have one structure, and format it in many ways.

Here is the same structure (newsletter name, date, lead article name, intro) formatted in three different ways.

Example 1:

The State of the Bullion

May 21, 2018

How to Buy Gold Today

You've been asking me, and asking me, "What's the best way to buy physical gold?"

Example 2:

THE STATE OF THE BULLION

May 21, 2018

HOW TO BUY GOLD TODAY

You've been asking me, and asking me, "What's the best way to buy physical gold?"

Example 3:

The State of the Bullion

May 21, 2018

HOW TO BUY GOLD TODAY

You've been asking me, and asking me, "What's the best way to buy physical gold?"

Summary:

Format is the way the text looks.

Structure is the arrangement of the elements in the text.

How formatting and structure have evolved

Let's take a look at the way that formatting and structure have developed since the earliest days of writing.

Early text had very little formatting, and no visible structure, aside from the way that the mason chiseled letters into the stone.

Inscription for Roman Consul Decius Marius Venantius Basilius in the Colosseum in Rome. Photo by WKnight94, under GFDL, via Wikimedia Commons

https://wikivisually.com/wiki/File:Rome_Colosseum_inscription _2.jpg#filehistory

The words written in scrolls often ran together, like this:

armavirumquecanotroiaequiprimusaboris

Isingofarmsandthemanwhofirstfromtheshoresof Troy

Vergil, *The Aeneid*

QUOUSQUETANDEMABUTERECATILINAPATIENTIANOSTRAQUAMDIUETI AMFURORISTETUUSNOSELUDETQUEMADFINEMSESEEFFRENATAIACTABI TAUDACIA

HOWMUCHLONGEROCATILINEWILLYOUABUSEOURPATIENCEHOWMUC HLONGERAREYOUGOINGTOMOCKUSWITHYOURMADNESSWHENISTHE RETOBEANENDOFYOURUNBRIDLEDAUDACITY

M. Tullius Cicero, *Against Catiline*

13

As you might expect, in those days, people had trouble reading.

In general, people ran their fingers under the text, saying the syllables out loud, and pausing to make sense out of the sound combinations.

How come?

- The text was one continuous stream. There were no spaces between words, no capital letters at the beginning of sentences, no periods at the end.

- On papyrus, the text was handwritten, so the handwriting of the scribe might be unusual or unfamiliar.

- The text often appeared in all capital letters, run together. So you had to work to figure out where one word ended, and the next began.

- At times the text ran left to right on one line, and then, like a plowman turning around in a field, it ran back from right to left. Greek name: *boustrophedon.*

- To save space and spare their wrists, scribes routinely abbreviated, leaving out the last syllables or vowels in common words.

Example: Julius Caesar amazed his soldiers and fellow Romans, because he could sight read.

- He could make sense of a text without saying it out loud.

- He did not use his finger to track his location in the row of characters.

To help their readers, scribes and writers came up with formatting and structure.

1. Writers invented white space so that readers could quickly distinguish one word from the next.

I sing of arms and the man who first from the shores of Troy

Other writers used dots or short lines to separate words.

2. To show where a section began, within the overall document, writers added headings.

Johannes Bockenheim, *Registrum coquinarie*, Nr. 28: Ad praeparandum agnum paschalem, MS Paris, B.N.F. by Otfried Lieberknecht http://expositions.bnf.fr/gastro/grands/171.htm

Headings help readers see when there is a break in the content. Headings announce what is to come. They clarify the structure of the material.

The heading's format and placement provide information about that section of the content, beyond the simple words in the heading.

3. Writers began to change the format of certain letters, to indicate the **start** of sentences. And they began to insert marks in the text to show the **end** of sentences.

- They distinguished between capital letters and lowercase letters, using the capital letters to set off the first words in sentences.

- They invented the period, or point—the first punctuation mark—to show that a sentence had come to an end.

Easy is the path leading down to hell, but long and hard the climb out.

15

4. Readers asked for another form of formatting to indicate structure: **Paragraphing**.

> To indicate the end of one section within the text and the start of the next, early writers inserted a mark that did not look like a letter. There was no agreement among the writers, so we see various marks, with no consistency, up to the earliest days of printing:
>
> - A wedge
>
> - A hook
>
> - A letter of the alphabet turned sideways
>
> - A short space after the last word of the paragraph
>
> - One, two, or three dots placed above the line at the end of the paragraph
>
> - The Greek letter gamma (which seems to have morphed into our current symbol for a paragraph ¶)
>
> In the Dark Ages and the Middle Ages, each scribe went his own way, using marks like these variously to indicate:
>
> - A section that might be dubious, or of doubtful provenance
>
> - A new person beginning to speak in a play
>
> - An exception
>
> - A summary
>
> - A new verse in a poem or in the Bible
>
> (See *The History of the* English *Paragraph*, by Edwin Herbert Lewis, University of Chicago Press, 1894.)
>
> During that same period, a few manuscripts show a slight indentation at the start of what we would call a paragraph, or a line of verse, or a line in the *Bible*.
>
> In the Renaissance, as printing came in, the indentation grew more popular as an indication of a paragraph.
>
> In all these ways, the writers, scribes, and printers were struggling with the idea that you could carve a text up into separate elements. Their many different attempts at creating a mark to indicate what we would call a new paragraph

eventually led to the convention of indenting the first line of the paragraph from the margin, and, sometimes, inserting extra space before each paragraph.

Easy is the path leading down to hell, but long and hard the climb out.

The ghost led me down past the caves, and the smoke, to the river Styx.

Charon, the boatman of the dead, poled out of the mist.

5. In the Middle Ages, some writers created marks to indicate that a series of items constituted a list.

The dingbats that we use to indicate the items in the list are a form of formatting, revealing information about the underlying structure.

Bullets help separate each item from all the others, while showing that all the items belong to the same group. In that way, bullets provide valuable information about the content.

The commons belong to the people.

- *They may run their cattle on the green.*
- *They may use the green for their dances.*
- *No man may fence in the commons.*
- *All souls tend the green equally.*

6. Readers responded to color, so the scribes sometimes used red to set off important information.

Scribes known as *rubricators* inserted text in red ink into the stream of text, to summarize what the next section would be about, to start the next section—or to set off the words of God. Like headings, these format changes helped readers recognize that the subject was changing.

Because every text was hand written, no one imagined that you could separate the content from its format or its structure. It all lived together on the physical page.

Printers codified markup.

The invention of printing separated the rough draft from the final printed copy. In between, markup was given its own life.

Before a printer could set type from the raw manuscript, or revise the type based on corrections to a proof, someone had to mark up the text.

Book Printing, by Daniel Chodowiecki, in public domain.

https://en.wikipedia.org/wiki/Woodblock_printing#/media/File: Chodowiecki_Basedow_Tafel_21_c_Z.jpg

Proofreader's marks started as a set of symbols or tags that told the person setting type how to format, organize, or edit the raw text. These marks indicated changes in spelling, wording, emphasis, weight, width, size, and slant, as well as indentation. For example, some marks said:

- Capitalize this letter.

- Insert space after this line.

- Delete this character.

- Make this phrase bold.

What makes something "proofreader's markup?"

- It is not part of the actual text. It stands apart from the flow of content, distinguishable from ordinary text.

- It will never be seen by the reader.

- It tells the type setter (or, in our day, the software) how to format, organize, or edit the text; in other words, it requests some operation on the text.

18

- It identifies pieces of text (a character, or set of characters) and meaningful elements (a heading, a title) within the document. It marks these distinct chunks of text.

What is NOT markup?

- The actual text that the reader will see.

- Images that the reader will see.

To make sure that the person casting the type understood what these marks meant, printers adopted a **common set** of scribbles.

Common Proofreader's Marks

Mark	What it means	How it looks	Result
	Delete	The layyout	The layout
	Close up	The ta ble	The table
	Capitalize	The mac	The Mac
	Lowercase	The Product	The product
	Insert	It is perhaps,	It is, perhaps,
	Transpose	You see can	You can see

Eventually, the set of proofreader's marks became standardized, so that everyone in the business knew them. In a way, the set can be thought of as a form of jargon: a **specialized vocabulary** for use by insiders. Eventually editors and writers adopted these marks, to correct proofs of their work.

This kind of markup helps us format individual words, sentences, paragraphs, columns, sections, pages, and whole documents.

And that formatting itself communicates information about the content, indicating answers to questions such as:

- What content is more important, or less?

- What content goes together, and what is separate?

- What text is an annotation, comment, or aside, and what content is the main event?

- What content ought to be deleted, moved, or inserted?

As printing became an industry, the thinking about markup changed. In the past, no one had actually thought of white space or paragraphing as "formatting." Writers and printers just used these tactics to help the readers.

But now that people were actually making marks on a manuscript, those marks became known as **markup**.

Some markup transformed the actual **content**—adding and deleting text, moving words around, inserting punctuation. So markup came to be seen as something **separate** from the original text.

Other markup told the printer how to **format** the text, making some of it italic, and other parts bold, for example.

Eventually, when printed in a book, the formatting would provide information *about* the content, indicating the relative importance and purpose of one chunk of text compared with another.

Gradually, people began to separate the notion of **format** and **structure** from the **markup**. Markup struck out on its own.

From hot type to cold

Proofreaders' marks followed the technology of printing.

When the Linotype machine appeared, the printers could type on a keyboard, and have the machine pour hot lead into molds and create slugs (lines of hot type), ready to place on the press.

The linotype operators continued to follow the proofreaders' marks, using levers and buttons on the machine to make the formatting changes, rather than selecting different individual wooden blocks from a case.

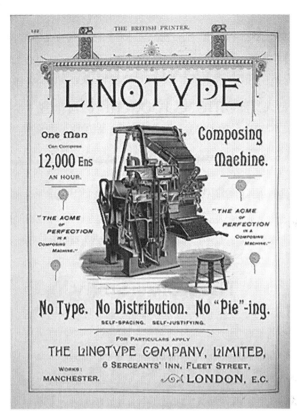

Advertisement in *The British Printer*, July-August 1891. Public domain: https://commons.wikimedia.org/wiki/File:Linotype_advert_in_the_Br itish_Printer.tiff

Schriftsetzer an einer Setzmaschine, Leipzig, by Roger Rossing, 1953, provided to Wikimedia Commons by the Deutsche Fotothek of the Saxon State Library / State and University Library Dresden (SLUB)

In the 1950s, when several computer companies were developing the software that we now call word processing applications, the engineers turned to the printing industry for advice on markup.

- The engineers conceived of text as a stream of characters.

- Inside that stream, they planned to insert markup.

- That markup would be placed inside special punctuation, known as delimiters, setting the markup off from the regular text.

- These units of markup would be called tags.

- Just as the linotype operator had to pull down a lever to start boldfacing a term, and then push the lever back up to stop boldfacing, the engineers figured that they would need a start tag at the beginning of the affected content, and an end tag at the end.

- The engineers therefore adapted the proofreaders' marks as tags, inventing text to replace the scribbles. In this way, the tag "{allcaps}" was invented to replace three lines drawn underneath the text. The programmers wrote software that would change the formatting of the text as each tag appeared.

The basic concept was that markup would appear as islands in the stream of text.

> I have learned to look on \<bf>nature\</bf>
> Not as in the hour of thoughtless youth, but
> Hearing oftentimes the still, sad music of
> \<i>humanity\</i>,
> Nor harsh nor grating, though of ample power
> to \<ul>chasten\</ul> and \<ul>subdue\</ul>.

The result of this markup:

> I have learned to look on **nature**
> Not as in the hour of thoughtless youth, but
> Hearing oftentimes the still, sad music of *humanity*,
> Nor harsh nor grating, though of ample power
> To chasten and subdue.

Each word-processing company invented its own set of tags.

During the 1970's, word processing machines sprang up everywhere. There were more than a hundred companies, each making its own proprietary hardware, with its own set of tags.

22

For any one format, there were dozens of different tags. For example, to start boldfacing the text, you had tags like these:

[bf]

[b}

|bold|

<bld>

~b~

As a result:

- People with different equipment could not easily share files.

- Large enterprises such as the Department of Defense had to spend millions of dollars to write code replacing all these proprietary tags with one tag, so that all the documents about a destroyer could be brought together and formatted in the same way by the same printing house.

- Publishing companies were getting manuscripts in a hundred different tag sets, and their printers were saying, "Just send us the files using the set of tags that we use, and we will be glad to print your book." So publishers too had to spend a lot of money to get a standard set of tags.

How IBM simplified markup

Customers were complaining about the chaos of tags, so an IBM team developed a way of bringing order to this mess.

They noticed that these word-processing machines could only do one thing—word processing—while a computer could be programmed to perform almost any function.

So Charles Goldfarb, Ed Mosher, and Ray Lorie came up with an approach that featured their initials: the Generalized Markup Language (GML) in 1969.

Their breakthrough idea:

Separate **content** and **structure** from **format**.

Their reasoning

1. Let's abstract the structure from the document.

- In business, most documents of a certain type follow the same structure.

- That structure can be described in an outline, a hierarchical list starting with the document itself at the top, and working down through chapters, sections, and so on to the lowest level, which might be a product name in a pricing table.

- When you look at the outlines of a hundred procedures, say, you can see that the structure is pretty much the same…if you describe each element in the abstract (a step, say) rather than the concrete instance ("Place the miter on the board.").

- So now we can build an abstract hierarchical list describing each element in all documents of this type.

- We can put that analysis in a separate file that describes that structure in terms that make sense to software, which tends to feed on hierarchical structures. We'll call that file a Document Type Definition.

- In that file, we will create a tag for each structural element, and we will define the relationship between the elements in the hierarchy. (A step belongs inside a procedure, for example, and an explanation follows a step). Now we have a set of tags that we can embed in the content, to label each element for the software (and, incidentally, for humans).

2. Let's reduce the content to a raw text file, with tags.

- There will be no formatting in this text file. Just ASCII text—content plus tags.

- We will insert a start tag in front of a structural element, and we will put one at the end. The tags will identify a step, or an explanation, but will not say how to format it.

- Because the file is raw text, any software can read it. It is not proprietary.

- To help the software, we will add a link to the Document Type Definition, the file that provides a formal description of the structure.

3. Let's separate the formatting from the content, and have software apply it later.

- The team noticed that book designers apply formatting to reveal the function, or purpose, of each structural element.

    Example: A step is more important than an explanation of a term inside the step, so a designer may make the step bold and 14 point, while indenting the explanation and putting it in 12 point text, without bolding. The design decisions are based on the purpose of each element, and its relationship to other elements.

- We can create a separate document called a stylesheet that tells software how to format each structural element. For each element, we will describe the formatting to apply. In this way, we can remove formatting from the file, and let software apply it later.

- By freeing the content from its format, we can apply several different style sheets to the same content, to publish our content on paper or on screen, in various sizes. We do not have to go through the whole document and reformat by hand.

With this approach, we end up with three documents, not one.

1. A Document Type Definition (DTD)

A description of the standard structure of a document in a particular genre, such as procedure, showing what its elements should be, in what order.

For each element, the document identifies a tag. For example, for a step, the Document Type Definition might say that the tag would be <step>.

2. A Stylesheet

A set of instructions to software telling it how to format each element.

The software, then, would look for that element's start tag, start formatting the element, and continue that formatting until it reached the end tag.

3. The content with tags

A file in plain text, containing the actual content **plus** tags. The tags surround and identify each element in the file.

Because the file is raw text, it has no formatting. There is nothing proprietary in this file, so almost any application can read it.

The content is just text. The tags are just text.

At the beginning of the file, an instruction says where software can find the Document Type Definition, to grasp the structure of the file. And another instruction says where the software can find the Stylesheet, to learn how to format each element.

Why is this called a markup language?

When you build the Document Type Definition, you can create any tags you want.

Yes, you have to follow a set of conventions for describing what those tags represent, and how they relate to each other in the hierarchical structure. In a way, these conventions form a **syntax**...a kind of grammar.

If you follow the rules of the grammar, you can create dozens, even hundreds of your own tags—a **vocabulary**.

By an act of imagination, the engineers called their invention a **language**. What they meant was that they had created a standard mechanism by which people could create sets of tags—vocabularies, if you will—that software could use to identify elements within a file.

And because the tags "marked up" the text, the engineers called their invention a markup language.

It's not a natural language. It is not even a specific set of tags. It is a mechanism for generating sets of tags in a way that software can use to identify (and therefore manipulate, and format) the elements within a file.

In what way is this a language?

The Document Type Definition follows a set of rules for generating a hierarchy of tags. Those rules derive from linguistics, going back to Panini's *Ashtadhyayi* (*The Eight Chapters*) circa 500 B.C.

- Panini invented a generative grammar, a set of algorithms for generating valid new words in Sanskrit. (See Vikram Chandra, *Geek Sublime*).

26

- Two professors of Sanskrit, Ferdinand de Saussure and Leonard Bloomfield, used Panini's ideas to launch modern linguistics.

- In 1959 John Backus, creator of the Fortran programming language, borrowed their metalinguistic formulae as a way describe a programming language.

- In creating the Document Type Definition, the IBM team used his method, known then as the Backus-Naur Form, to describe the way that you can create a set of words known as tags, in a hierarchy that follows a standard set of rules—rules that software can "understand" so that it "recognizes" the structure and the tags.

Following these rules, we create a Document Type Definition, which describes the standard structure of every document of a particular type. This structure is sometimes known as a **content model**.

- A content model is essentially an outline.

- In that outline, we see DOCUMENT at the top, and then within that, elements such as TITLE, AUTHOR, INTRODUCTION, ABSTRACT, OVERVIEW, PROCEDURE, APPENDIX, GLOSSARY.

- The model names and describes each element.

- The model puts those elements in order. You have to have a title before you have an introduction, for example.

- The model says which elements are required (such as TITLE) and which ones are optional (such as APPENDIX).

In the Document Type Definition, then, we have an annotated list of all the elements that may or must be used in a certain type of document. So the content model tells us what tags we can use to mark up our content.

In this way, we can see that as a language, the Generalized Markup Language (like its grandchild, XML) is **unnatural**.

- The Document Type Definition (DTD) describes a set of tags in a way that both humans and software can "read."

- Each set of tags can be thought of as a specialized vocabulary.

- Because the tags are usually terms that make sense to human beings, we call them "meaningful," or "semantic." We are inventing and defining a small set of words—but in a very constricted, formal way, quite unlike the way that ordinary people invent new words in a natural language.

27

- Because the DTD describes those tags in structural terms (how they are organized, how they relate to each other), software can build a model of the structure of that type of document, and then navigate the document from tag to tag.

- Other software can come in and use the same model to apply formatting to the elements marked by those tags.

This idea of a markup language caught on.

IBM's Generalized Markup Language got extraordinary interest (and payments) from large customers such as

- The U.S. Department of Defense

- The American Library Association

- The American Association of Publishers

- Industries such as trucking and aerospace

With their input, the Generalized Markup Language grew in complexity, and in 1974, it morphed into the Standard Generalized Markup Language (SGML).

Like GML, SGML gives you a set of conventions that let you generate a set of tags in a carefully defined structure. But despite the name, SGML has some limitations.

- SGML is not a set of tags. You might think of it as a machine for generating tags.

- It is not really a language; it is more like a grammar or syntax for putting together units of a very controlled vocabulary, spawning meaningful units that we call tags.

- It is not a programming language, because tags do not perform any function. They just sit there. Software comes into the file, looks at the tags, and does stuff. But the tags themselves do not act.

- It is generalized, because the Document Type Definition describes a general situation—what the typical document should contain, not what a particular document does contain. The DTD describes a class of documents. Any particular document is just one instance of that class.

- It is a standard, because it sets up conventions that many different software vendors can adopt, to exchange data without a hiccup. But it does not enforce any particular set of tags, or any particular software.

SGML Benefits

- Consistent organization and format for large-scale paper publications (aircraft maintenance, nuclear power, telecommunications, space)

- Persistence for long-lasting documents, going through many revisions, updates, cross references

- Consistent content, through a single source of raw text that you can publish in many media

SGML Drawbacks

- Extremely complex

- Aimed at publishing, not processing

- Not lightweight enough for the web. (Shucks, back in 1974, even the Internet was still a dream).

- Hard to implement

- Overstuffed with too many options, so the software to process an SGML document gets big and complicated.

Tim Berners-Lee used SGML to create HTML (1989).

The Hypertext Markup Language (HTML) is really just one Document Type Definition written in SGML. It defines one set of tags, for elements such as H1 for Level One Headings, and P for paragraph. It has been expanded to accommodate more flexible and more precise formatting of Web pages.

What HTML tags say

- This is a heading.

- This is a paragraph.

- This is a table.

- This is the anchor for a link. If someone clicks it, the browser should follow the path to this other page.

HTML Pluses

- Flexible enough for most formats

- Easily written in a text editor or web design software

- Raw, because HTML files are regular text files, making for faster transmission, low overhead, and portability

HTML Minuses

- HTML tags do not identify meaningful content. Yes, it is a heading, but what is the heading about?

- Without semantic information (what kind of content does this element contain, what does it mean?) it is hard to tell software how to manipulate the element in a meaningful way. That is, you cannot say, "Boldface each step," because the tags do not tell the software which content is a step. Each step may just appear as another <p>.

- E-commerce demands database exchanges, and HTML takes a lot of massaging to get data in and out of databases. An HTML page is not designed to map easily to a record in a database.

- In the early days, everyone wrote HTML badly, so browser companies made their parsers extremely forgiving...which meant that there was a lot of code in there on how to deal with clumsy tagging. The parser became huge. It would not fit on mobile devices. (A parser analyzes the tags to verify that they have been entered correctly).

- The growth of HTML tended to focus on formatting, not semantics (that is, not on what the elements were about, what they **meant**). Tim Berners-Lee had deliberately made HTML very bland and generic, so that it could be used in many circumstances. But as a result, software could not tell the difference between one <p> (having, say, a step) and another <p> (holding, say, an explanation).

Because HTML focused on format more than meaningful structure, and because it was so clumsy in dealing with databases and the web, a group got together to simplify SGML, and aim it entirely at the web.

XML launched in 1996, and became a standard in 1998.

XML is a subset of SGML. Any SGML processor can read XML. But not every Web browser can handle XML straight, so at the last minute a web server often has to translate the page into HTML for older browsers.

Like SGML, XML separates format, content, and structure.

- The Document Type Definition defines the abstract structure for this type of document, creating a vocabulary and organization of tags.

- The document itself uses those tags to label the actual content.

- A stylesheet tells the browser what format to apply to the content, using those tags.

What XML says

- Use this content model (Document Type Definition or schema).

- Use this stylesheet.

- This document is a catalog.

- This is a book description.

- This is the book's title.

- This is the book's page count.

- This is the book's price, in USD.

- This is the book's ISBN.

XML Pluses

- XML is designed for use on the Internet.

- XML makes it easy to write programs that manipulate the content of XML documents.

- XML keeps the number of options down, so processing software such as parsers can be lightweight.

- XML documents can be read by humans.

- XML is a methodical and precise language, and therefore unambiguous.

- XML documents map exactly to a database schema, so that all database systems can easily import an XML document, or take values from its own records, and export those as XML.

XML Minuses

- The formal language for building a Document Type Definition uses Extended Backus-Naur Form (EBNF), which takes a while to get used to.

- You can create any tags you want to, but you also have to define a standard structure for those elements (a DTD or schema).

- Because the standard uses some punctuation marks as delimiters, setting tags off from the surrounding text, you have to use substitutes

31

(known as entity references) that point to the characters such as *greater than*, *less than*, and *ampersand*. If the document is valid, the parser replaces the entity references with the real characters before passing the text along to the browser.

XML as a language vs the Hypertext Markup Language, as a language

- XML is a standard for creating sets of tags. Like SGML, it is a mechanism, a machine, you might say, for creating sets of tags.

- HTML is just one set of tags, built in XML's parent, SGML. The Document Type Definition defining this set of tags comes with every web browser, so it can "understand" the tags and apply some formatting to the content, based on those tags. (An H1 is bigger than an H2).

XML tagging vs HTML tagging

- In XML you must have end tags. In HTML, you should have end tags, but the browser has a tool called a parser that forgives you if you forget. To keep its code small and lightweight, the XML parser does not forgive.

- In XML, all elements must be properly nested. (A step must appear inside a procedure, not outside; you must close one step before you start another).

- In XML, capitalization matters. You cannot match a <p> start tag with a </P> end tag.

- In XML, attribute values must always appear inside quotes, after an equal sign.

- You need to use straight quotes, not curly quotes.

Good news: If you have been writing XHTML, you have been following the conventions of XML.

XML files are text files.

- Proprietary files can only be opened by certain software, not all. XML files are not proprietary. They are just text files.

- Text files can be read by almost any program.

- Markup just adds metadata, making the text file "self describing."

XML is **extensible**.

- Any company can create its own tags and structures.

- Those tags and structures are open to anyone else to read and manipulate. They are not proprietary, secret, or hidden.

- Industries can adopt standard vocabularies. Businesses can have their own variations, and easily translate back and forth.

XML describes a **tree**.

- Each document has a root element. Oddly, that element sits at the top of the hierarchy, and all other content flows down from it.

- The structure of the document is a tree, not a network, not a table, not an unrolling scroll or flowing stream of text.

- Elements have parent/child relationships.

- Elements that have children are called branches; those without children are the leaves.

XML works well with databases.

An XML document has a well-defined hierarchy, such as:

Procedure

    Title

    Short Description

    Steps

Similarly, a database record can have a well-defined hierarchy, with the same names as the elements. In this example, each record is a Procedure. The fields are

    Title

    Short Description

    Steps

The database software uses the tags in the XML document to figure out where to find the values for these fields—the content. The text between the start tag for Title and the end tag for Title is the value that the database system puts into the Title field. And so on.

You build the Document Type Definition to map to the database, and you build the database to map to the structure described in the DTD. Then

33

you can pull values from the XML document and put them in the database, or retrieve values from the database and put them into an XML document.

What good is this? You do not have to store the document as a document. You can store separate elements in a database.

That way, you can use a different DTD, and pull out only a subset of the elements you used before. For example, if you are writing a job aid, you might only pull out the Title and Steps, leaving out the Short Description.

Examples

Example of an XML markup of a marketing article

```
<?xml version='1.0' encoding='UTF-8'
standalone='no'?>
<?xml-stylesheet type='txt/css'
href='featuresandbenefits.css'>
<!DOCTYPE featuresandbenefits SYSTEM
''http://www.theprices.com/
special/featuresandbenefits.dtd''>
<featuresandbenefits>
<challenge> Today, even a small
business needs a web site. To make it
easy for customers to find out about
your products, see testimonials from
other satisfied customers, or get a
map to your store, you need a web
site.</challenge>
<solution>The PR Express offers a fast
and easy way to build a web site that
expresses your business
case.</solution>
</featuresandbenefits>
```

Example DTD

```
<!ELEMENT featuresandbenefits
(challenge, solution)>
<!ELEMENT challenge (#PCDATA)>
<!ELEMENT solution (#PCDATA)>
```

Example XSLT stylesheet

```
<?xml version=''1.0''>
<xsl:stylesheet
xmlns:xsl=''http://www.w3.org/TR/WD-
xsl''>
<xsl:output method=''xml''
version=''1.0''
encoding=''windows-1252'' omit-xml-
declaration=''no'' indent=''yes''/>
<xsl:template match=''/''>
<xsl:for-each
select=''featuresandbenefits''>
<SPAN STYLE=''font-
style:italic''></SPAN>
</xsl:for-each>
</xsl:template>
</xsl:output>
</xsl:stylesheet>
```

Example Screen Display

Today, even a small business needs a web site. To make it easy for customers to find out about your products, see testimonials from other satisfied customers, or get a map to your store, you need a web site.

The PR Express offers a fast and easy way to build a web site that expresses your business case.

Where you fit in

As a writer, you may work with a programming team to create the Document Type Definition or schema. (A schema is another version of the content model, written in XML itself).

- You identify the common elements that show up in every document of a certain type, such as a product data sheet, or a procedure.

- You give those elements meaningful names.

- You decide which ones are required, and which are optional.

- You tell the team what order these elements must appear in.

- You specify which elements can be repeated, such as steps in a procedure, and which ones can only show up once per document, such as the TITLE.

You may consult with a designer to suggest formats for each element.

- The designer writes a stylesheet, saying what each element ought to look like.

- The web browser will use the stylesheet to format each element.

You use an XML editor of some kind to write a document.

- You tell the software where to find the Document Type Definition.

- The software tells you which elements you can write in which order.

- As you write, you create one element after another, and the software surrounds your content with the right tags.

- You also tell the software what stylesheet to use, so it can display the content the way an end user will see it.

- You can also switch to a view of the actual tags, if you like.

- You submit your document to some form of content management software, which stores it in a database, and, when necessary, publishes it.

The reader uses a web browser to view your document.

1. A utility known as a parser reads the document, to find out what Document Type Definition to fetch, brings that down, reads it, and compares it with the document.

2. If the parser finds that the tags in the document correctly match the ones in the DTD, in the right order, it passes the document along to the browser.

3. The browser fetches the stylesheet mentioned in the start of the document, and applies those formats to the elements, then displays the formatted document on screen.

I admit it: Writing in XML feels odd!

- You have to think structurally more than you did in "unstructured" programs like Word. You have to be more aware of the sequence of elements: Which one is allowed next? Where should I put this new information? What is the function of this particular element?

- You do not create the set of tags. A team does that. Yes, as a writer, you might be a member of the team, giving advice about the standard structure of documents of a particular type, such as a procedure. But you would work with an information architect, a designer, and probably a programmer. And you will only be put on a team like that when you have had a lot of experience with the organization's documents, so you can talk about what is common, what is required, what is optional, and so on. Deciding on a new set of tags takes months of negotiation, because so many people will have to use them.

- You do not have to insert the tags yourself, because an XML editor does that for you. (Purists write in a text editor such as Notepad or TextEdit, inserting every tag). But no matter what tool you are using, you do have to **memorize** the standard structure of each type of content, whether that is a product data sheet, or a procedure. As you move from one element to the next, when you write, you need to have the standard structure—the content model—firmly in mind. Think of it as a template, an outline to be filled in. The goal is to present the same kind of information in the same type of element all the time, across all writers and all documentation, so that users can figure out where to look for that information, or realize, hey, I can skip this element.

- **Re-using** standard content takes a little getting used to. As writers, we may crib a paragraph here and there from our own work, but if we grab something from another person's documents, we rarely resist the urge to tinker…improving the prose style, for example, or tweaking the first sentence so that it fits into the flow of the section. You can't do that when you re-use content. You tell the XML editor to ask the content management system for an element such as a

37

concept topic describing the routers in a certain product line; the database serves up that boilerplate, and you tell the XML editor to insert it. Essentially, the editor is inserting a pointer to that paragraph, out in the database. Therefore, later, if marketing changes the product name, it gets changed once, and in a nanosecond, the change miraculously appears in your document.

- **Reading** an XML document, you can get tripped up by all the tags. Good news: after a while, you learn to skip all the tags and read the good stuff, that is, the actual content that lives **between** the tags. And most of the time, you can write in a WHAT YOU SEE IS WHAT YOU GET environment, just like a regular word processing program. You only switch to the tag view if you want to see what's going on there. At that point, you can get valuable information from the tags, because they describe each element in a meaningful way—this is where the ISBN number should go, this is where the publication date should go, and so on. In that way, the tags serve as reminders of what content you should insert.

- You lose the ability to **cheat**. You cannot get away with fudging a margin, changing the line spacing, reducing a font size just to get more on a page. The stylesheet forbids it.

- You cannot just insert stray facts **anywhere**. Each element answers a particular user question. So when you find an answer, you have to figure out which element is designed to serve as a container for that answer. That's where it goes.

- **Editing goes faster**. You become merciless. If the content does not belong in the element, out it goes. For example, a step must tell the user what to do. If the writer has placed background information into a step, out it goes.

- Overall, you have to **abandon** the habits of the book. You do not need chapter openers, descriptions of what you will talk about next, transitions, summaries. Each chunk of content lives on its own, without reference to anything that might have come before, or that you might expect to come later.

- Your style becomes **staccato**. No smooth music here. You are essentially filling out fields in a form, one after another. Once you get familiar with writing in this way, you can make the tone sound friendly, even easy to understand. But music it is not.

- At first you may feel like a robot. But think of the **payoff**.

- You give up some originality of structure, so that your user can become more successful in navigating, discovering, understanding, and using your information. Your writing, then, becomes less personal, so that it can be processed by software, in the service of **your users**.

XML solves many problems

Because we are now able to identify individual elements within an XML document, we can think in terms of pieces of content, not just complete documents. We are outgrowing a document orientation.

We are creating content that can be assembled into a wide variety of publications, pages, knowledge base topics, help systems, discussion forums, chatbots, push emails, and automated newsfeeds. Each publication grabs just the elements it needs. XML makes this possible, because each element has a tag that tells the software what kind of content it contains—a step, say, or an explanation. So you can say, just pull all the steps, and leave the explanations behind, for a new job aid.

Content management software makes it possible to store all the elements in a single database, then dole them out as needed to different publications, for different devices, for different audiences.

In this way, XML helps us solve many of the problems we have inherited from a world of documents.

Problem #1: Inconsistency

Right now, many web pages, documents, and even emails are inconsistently organized and chaotically formatted. The company may put standards in a style guide, but no one really has to follow them. Inconsistency of structure from page to page, from department to department, slows down users when they want to navigate, discover, understand, and use the content.

Variations in style and structure, across the site, also mar the brand.

Solution: Create consistent structure based on the content model, and consistent formatting based on the stylesheet

- Consistency reinforces the brand—that constellation of characteristics, values, and ideas that we promise to deliver in every conversation, transaction, or interaction that a person has with us. But the benefits of consistent branding go beyond marketing to help users grasp the fact that they are still on the same site, using the same company's products, hearing from the same corporate voice. Like a logo, a strong brand makes the site cohere for the user.

- Using a standard Document Type Definition or schema and a standard stylesheet guarantees that each document of that type will look like all the others, and follow the same structure. Thus, when someone has read one of these documents, that person is prepared to read the others. Familiarity with the structure and format helps speed that person to the right information in another document.

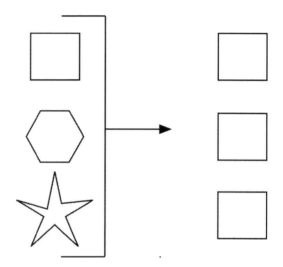

- Consistency reassures the readers that we are one company and know what we are doing.

Problem #2: Some information gets out of date in some places, updated elsewhere.

With a big collection of documents, updating can be erratic, difficult to manage. In a particular book or web page, one or two facts get out of date, but we have no way of tracking that, discovering that. Updating tends to wait on a new release, just as we used to wait for a new edition of the book, instead of doing continuous fixes. In documents, then, we have months or years of increasing obsolescence, a moment of currency, and another long period of decline.

Solution: Update once, publish everywhere

With XML we can tell our XML editor to find all references to the old product name, in the content management system's database, then correct them all at the same time.

40

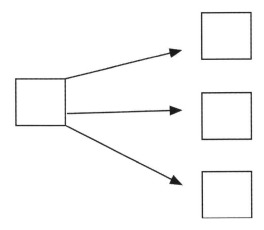

Problem # 3: Re-inventing the wheel

In a document world, the elements of one page cannot easily be reused elsewhere. At best we can copy, paste, and revise the material, adjusting it for the new context.

Solution: Re-use the same content everywhere.

- With an XML editor we can find that other paragraph, and pop it in, whole. Faster, even if the effect is a bit staccato.

- Reuse saves money. In some companies, half the information in the manuals is almost the same, or exactly the same. XML allows us to say, OK, if you are writing about yet another router, and you are saying the same thing as in every other manual about routers, do not write new stuff: Re-use that element.

- We can use exactly the same element in many locations without rewriting it.

- We can search for a set of elements by tag (Give me all the elements called <product_name> in this chapter).

- We can take apart an existing element and use selected components, but not others, in a new object.

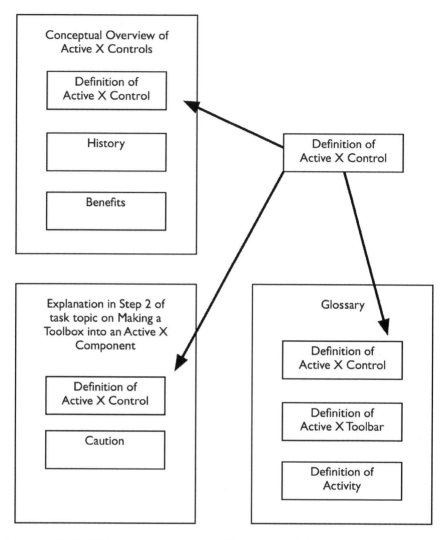

Problem #4: We cannot easily provide different information to different groups.

- It is hard to customize content for a particular type of user when you can only offer whole documents.

- One document often contains information aimed at different groups...from beginners to experts, from techies to administrators.

- In some organizations, you have to write separate documents for each major audience. Inevitably you are going to repeat a lot of the information, but in a document world, that is the price you pay for customization.

Solution: Customize content for groups, personalize for individuals.

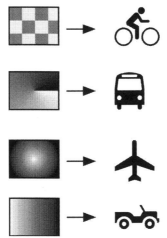

You can deliver different travel info depending on what mode of transportation the user prefers.

- With XML, you can set up a template for each type of user, and draw information from the database, one element at a time. In that way, you can dish out different content to people whose profile shows that they are in different groups, such as technicians or managers.

- Similarly, you can offer individuals a personalized set of content.

- Because you are dealing with content, not documents, you can assemble elements on the fly to create customized content.

- Customization lets us address small groups, with particular content relevant to them.

- Personalization demands that we break up our content into objects, so individuals can decide exactly what goes into their material.

- Customer Relationship Management programs can track individual visitors by their cookies, and offer personal welcome pages, with focused content, including topics that the person has indicated an interest in, mentions of products that the person owns, awareness of that person's previous transactions.

- XML offers content that can be broken up and reused in many different situations, making personalization and customization possible.

Problem #5: Users cannot find the information that they need in documents.

- In a document world, users ask specific questions, but get general answers (large documents, with the answer on page 357).

- Document sizes become unwieldy, as we cram thousands of related sections into the same volume, bursting its binding. What we gain in the convenience of a single volume begins to slip away under the inconvenience of browsing or searching through this pile.

- Skimming and scanning are difficult because the material has not been divided up into discrete chunks with enough subheads.

- Following the convention of a book, the menu system may offer only one way into the material, so users cannot follow their own mental models, discovering a particular chunk of information at the bottom of their own paths.

- Searches cannot be targeted at a particular type of information (this topic, within instructions, but not conceptual overviews).

- Even advanced searches do not let users see anything smaller than a document. So their hits are all whole documents, each covering dozens, hundreds, or thousands of topics beyond the one the users are looking for.

- Links do not always take users to the information that they want to find, but dump them at the top of a large page, with a cheery "Good luck!"

Solution: Offer advanced search using metadata.

We can improve searches by letting users use metadata to refine or narrow an advanced search.

Each element in XML may come with one or more **attributes**. Each attribute describes the content of the element. An attribute has two parts, a name (such as *natural language*) and a value (such as *English*).

We call these attributes and their values "metadata," because they are **about** the data. The attributes are hidden from the user but available to a search mechanism, because they are embedded inside the start tags for the elements.

Example attributes:

- Genre

- Subject

- Owner of the information

- Date created or modified

- Subject Matter Experts or Authors

- Products named

- Product ID

- Natural language used in the writing

- Programming language used in the software being discussed

- Operating systems this product runs on

An advanced search offers users the chance to search for a term, date, or number, in a specific field, such as Product ID, or Natural Language. Essentially, these attribute values allow the user to filter out the irrelevant, and focus on the specific information wanted.

Problem #6: We waste time and money rewriting, reformatting, editing.

Copying and pasting costs money. Rewriting because we cannot borrow from an older document wastes time. Constantly having to reformat what we steal drives us crazy.

Solution: Use XML to save the company money because...

- You can reuse a lot of content without taking the time to rewrite or edit it.

- You can enforce standard structures through software.

- You can ensure that all documents are formatted the same way.

- You can create new tag sets as needed.

- You can speed up the publication process.

Problem #7: Users want fast facts.

Impatient, upset, angry, anxious, users come to our content with a job to do. They are not settling back in an armchair to read 300 pages of our prose.

Solution: Use XML to give the user...

- The ability to filter the search results to focus on a particular language, product line, type of content.

- Greater interactivity with even the smallest chunks of the material

- More precise personalization

- Consistent structure of documents of the same type, so that after reading one, the user can quickly navigate the next.

- Consistent formatting, to help the user in the same way.

- Focused content, because each element contains only information that answers a particular type of question.

- No transitions, rambling introductions, or detours. Each chunk of content, that is, each element, has its own purpose, and anything irrelevant to that purpose gets cut.

Historical artifact: The XML Manifesto

In creating XML the team set out these design goals.

- XML shall be straightforwardly usable over the Internet.

- XML shall support a wide variety of applications.

- XML shall be compatible with SGML.

- It shall be easy to write programs which process XML documents.

- The number of optional features in XML is to be kept to the absolute minimum, ideally zero.

- XML documents should be human-legible and reasonably clear.

- The XML design should be prepared quickly.

- The design of XML shall be formal and concise.

- XML documents shall be easy to create.

- Terseness in XML markup is of minimal importance.

https://www.w3.org/TR/REC-xml/

Prolog

Most XML documents start with a prolog. To understand why, we need to adopt an XML perspective.

Getting into the XML mindset

When we use a pen to jot down a shopping list on the back of envelope, the content ("kale," "bleach," "chips," say) is indistinguishable from the structure (a list of items, arranged in the order of the aisles in our supermarket) and the formatting (our elegant penmanship).

The three aspects of our hand-written document are **inseparable**.

But when we are working in the land of XML, we must separate our **content** from a description of the elements in the **structure** and a set of rules for **formatting** those elements.

Content, structure, format…each gets its own **file**:

- The content and tags go into the **actual XML document**.

- The descriptions of the elements and their tags, and their hierarchical relationships, go into the **Document Type Definition** (DTD) or a schema.

- The rules for formatting those elements go into a **stylesheet**.

The XML document points to the DTD and stylesheet, both of which describe the elements in the XML document.

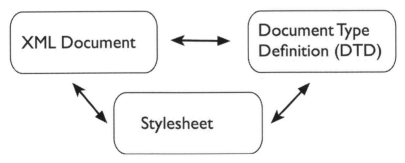

How do we tie these together?

We tie them together by starting the XML document with a **prolog**. We use the prolog to list **standards** and **files** that exist outside of the document, so that software can find them.

The prolog points to:

- The **version** of XML that we are using

- The **character set** that we are using (such as English or Chinese)

- The **Document Type Definition** that describes the elements in this document

- The **stylesheet** that says how the browser should format those elements

The prolog is separate from the body of the XML file. The user never sees the prolog. It contains no content.

But the prolog serves the programs that process all these documents, putting everything together so that a nicely formatted document appears on the user's screen.

The prolog introduces the XML document—for software.

An XML document may have three parts: the prolog, body, and epilog. Of these three parts, only the body has content that human beings will read.

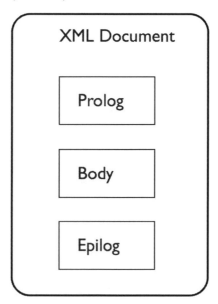

Of these three, the only required part is the **body**. But you usually need a **prolog** too, so that software can "read" and prepare the document for display. But you never need an **epilog**.

Most XML documents, then, contain a **prolog** and a **body**.

Example of a complete XML document

The first three paragraphs form the prolog of this document.

The rest of the lines starting with <booklist> form the body,

```
<?xml version='1.0' encoding='UTF-8'
standalone='no' ?>
<!DOCTYPE BookList SYSTEM
"http://www.gobi.org/booklist.dtd">
<?xml-stylesheet type='txt/css'
href='booklist.css'?>

<booklist>
   <book>
       <title>The Best of Online
       Shopping
       </title>
       <author>Lisa and Jonathan Price
       </author>
       <pages>500</pages>
       <price>$16.00</price>
       </book>
<!--More books to come, soon.-->
</booklist>
```

Q: Why have a prolog separate from the body?

A: To separate information aimed primarily at software from the actual content of the document, aimed (mostly) at people.

The prolog contains information that will be useful to two programs: the parser and the browser.

- The **parser** acts like your English teacher back in high school, analyzing every character in the document, to make sure everything is correct, according to the rules of XML.

- If so, the **browser** program looks at the stylesheet to find out how to format the content in the body, then displays the formatted content on your screen.

How it works on your device

An XML file arrives on your device. Here's what happens next.

1. When the XML file lands on your device, the web browser assigns a piece of software called the Parser to analyze the incoming file.

2. The Parser reads the prolog, notes the version of XML, consults that standard, and checks that the tags have been written correctly (the document is "well formed") according to that version of XML.

    (If not, the Parser stops, and refuses to have anything more to do with the document. On that news, the browser may refuse to display the document, or it may display the document as raw text.)

3. If the XML document is indeed well formed, the Parser returns to the prolog, finds the pointer to the Document Type Definition, fetches that document, and checks that the tags in the XML document map to the Document Type Definition. (If so, the document is "valid.")

    (If the document is not valid, in any way, no matter how trivial, the Parser tells the Browser not to bother trying to format it, because the element tags may not match those that the stylesheet expects— the ones described in the Document Type Definition.)

4. If the document is well formed and valid, the Parser sends it to the Browser for "rendering," that is, preparing it for display.

5. The Browser's "rendering engine" reads the prolog, finds the pointer to the stylesheet, fetches the stylesheet, and applies it to the body of the document, formatting the elements according to the rules in the stylesheet.

6. Success! The Browser displays the nicely formatted content.

All the content is there, and it is formatted. But the user does not see any of the tags, or the prolog, or the Document Type Definition, or the stylesheet. All of those things are hidden behind the scenes.

What's in the Document Type Definition (DTD)?

The DTD defines the standard structure of every document of this type. For example, if the document is a procedure, the DTD describes the elements needed, such as prerequisites and steps, and specifies how they will be arranged, in what order, in all such documents.

The goals:

- **Consistency** of structure across all documents of this type

- Ability to identify **one particular element** or set of elements, such as steps, for special formatting, or for reuse

- Ability to **filter a search** for a particular element type, such as the names of procedures

- Ability to **select** only the elements that a particular person or group might be interested in, as when experts ask for just the steps, with no explanatory text.

The DTD defines the structure.

The DTD describes the structure of the standard content of this type of document.

- The structure is a **hierarchy**. At the top is the genre itself, such as Concept Topic, or Task Topic. At the bottom are the smallest pieces of content, such as a product name or a store location ZIP code.

- Each type of content is considered an **element** in the structure. (For example, every instruction is a COMMAND element).

- An element can be considered a **class**, that is, a category of content. When you write the actual XML document, you create a particular **instance** of that class, filling it with your own special content.

- Each element in that hierarchy gets its own **tag**. (For example, every step in a procedure is of the type *step*, so it starts with the tag <step>.)

- Some elements are **required**, and some are **optional**.

- An element may occur **once** or **many times.** Or if it is optional, it may **never** actually show up in a particular XML document.

- An element may **contain** other elements, nested within it. Thus, an element called STEP might contain COMMAND as a required element, and INFO ELEMENT, and NOTE, both optional.

- In turn, any element may be **contained** within one or more other elements.

The DTD describes the **order** in which the elements must or may appear. For example, you might have rules like these:

- A **title** must appear before an **introduction**.

- If you are going to explain a term that appears in the command, that optional info element must appear **after** the command.

In this way the DTD provides an abstract outline of the standard document, naming the types of content, but not providing any of the actual content. It is a model for all the documents of this type, a skeleton waiting for flesh.

Sample DTD

```
<!ELEMENT memo (to,from,heading,body)>
<!ELEMENT to (#PCDATA)>
<!ELEMENT from (#PCDATA)>
<!ELEMENT heading (#PCDATA)>
<!ELEMENT body (#PCDATA)>
```

This DTD says that in a standard memo, there must be a TO section before the FROM section, and both of those appear before a HEADING, and that appears before the BODY.

Each of those elements contains something called Parsed Character Data, which we know as regular text.

Here is a document that follows this standard structure.

```
<?xml version="1.0"?>
<!DOCTYPE memo SYSTEM "memo.dtd">
<memo>
<to>Dev Team</to>
<from>Alyssa</from>
<heading>Hour sheets due</heading>
<body>Remember to send me your time
sheets by 4 p.m. on Friday. </body>
</memo>
```

Another example

We start with an outline of the content—a rough content model.

```
Artwork
    Title
    Year
    Artist
    Medium
    Size
            Height
            Width
            Units
    Signature
            Name
```

Date
Signature Location
Signature Description
Description
Institution
Collection
Acquisition
Donor
Accession Number
Image

Based on the outline, we build a DTD:

```
<!ELEMENT artwork (title, year,
artist, medium, size, signature,
description, institution, collection,
acquisition, image)>
<!ELEMENT title>
<!ELEMENT year>
<!ELEMENT artist>
<!ELEMENT medium>
<!ELEMENT size (height, width, units)
>
<!ELEMENT height>
<!ELEMENT width>
<!ELEMENT units>
<!ELEMENT signature (name, date,
signaturelocation,
signaturedescription) >
<!ELEMENT name>
<!ELEMENT date>
<!ELEMENT signaturelocation>
<!ELEMENT signaturedescription>
<!ELEMENT description>
<!ELEMENT institution>
<!ELEMENT collection>
<!ELEMENT acquisition (donor.
accessionnumber) >
<!ELEMENT donor>
<!ELEMENT accessionnumber>
<!ELEMENT image>
```

Here is an XML document based on that DTD:

```
<?xml version="1.0"?>
<!DOCTYPE artwork SYSTEM
"artwork.dtd">
<?xml-stylesheet type='txt/css'
href='artcatalog.css'?>

<artwork>
<title>Pie Seller</title>
<year>1877</year>
<artist>Charles Hindley</artist>
<medium>Engraving on paper</medium>
<size>
   <height>3</height>
   <width>3.3</width>
   <units>inches</units>
</size>
<signature>
   <name>C. Hindley</name>
   <date>1877</date>
   <signaturelocation>verso
   </signaturelocation>
   <signaturedescription> gray ink
   </signaturedescription>
</signature>
<description>A Londoner selling
custard pies. </description>
<institution>The Pie
Institute</institution>
<collection> Cries of London
Collection</collection>
<acquisition>
   <donor>Association of London Pastry
   Chefs</donor>
   <accessionnumber>1994.1336</accessio
   nnumber>
</acquisition>
<image>pieseller01</image>
</artwork>
```

Here is that content displayed with formatting applied by the stylesheet.

Title: Pie Seller

Date: 1877

Artist: Charles Hindley

Medium: Etching on paper

Size: 3 x 3.3 inches

Signature: C. Hindley. 1877 (verso, gray ink)

Description: A Londoner selling custard pies.

Institution: The Pie Institute

Collection: Cries of London

Gift of Association of London Pastry Chefs

Accession Number: 1994.1336

The DTD defines the attributes of the elements.

Each element may have one or more **attributes**—categories of information that must or may be provided **about** the element for the use of staff, search engines, or other software.

Example

If you have a concept topic describing a feature in a new product, you may need to include information about the author, date of creation, and natural language. That information is not displayed to the user, but it is used by the administrators and authors in the system. (Where are the concept topics I wrote in the last month?)

The DTD defines each attribute for an element:

- Each attribute has a **name**, such as Natural_Language.

- Each attribute must have some kind of **value**, such as French.

- The DTD describes **what kind** of numbers or text can serve as the value. (The author will fill this information in when creating the XML document).

The DTD may also describe entities.

If the standard document of this type includes non-textual elements, such as a company logo, or characters in a foreign language, the DTD gives those things names, and tells software where to find the files or the standards.

These items are considered entities because they exist outside of the XML file, like protoplasmic beings in space. When you write a particular document, you tell your XML editor to bring them into the document as needed.

You do not have to create the DTD yourself.

Usually, you get handed the DTD. As a writer, your job is to understand the standard structure, which is a lot easier than building the actual DTD.

When you start to write an XML document, you tell the XML editor where to find the DTD, and it uses that to tell you what elements you may create, in what order. You can write while looking at the actual tags, or you can switch to the WHAT YOU SEE IS WHAT YOU GET view, like in a word processing program, hiding the tags behind the scenes. (The XML editor applies whatever stylesheet you are assigned, putting a path to it in the prolog).

An alternative approach: The schema

There are two main ways to describe the standard structure of a particular genre—a Document Type Definition, and a schema.

The older approach is the DTD. Invented as part of SGML, the DTD was born before XML even existed, and it is widely supported even today. But it has some limitations.

- When you create a field in a database, you can require that the values entered conform to some constraint. A Date field must have a date. A number field must have a number. So if you are moving information back and forth between an XML document and a database, you'd like to have the XML document enforce those rules. But a DTD does not offer the wide range of constraints that a database does. So software cannot assure a database that the incoming data is valid, field by field.

- In a database, we can make sure that some elements, such as the Social Security field, contain unique information. In other words, we want to make sure that we are not assigning the same number to two different people. Compared with a database, the DTD has only limited methods for validating that a particular element is unique.

- When defining a large, complex document, we often want to re-use some material over and over. In a DTD, you can define those rules in one place, and reuse them elsewhere, but not easily.

- The DTD itself is not written in XML, so it cannot easily be modified in an XML editor, the tool that we most often use when working on XML documents.

To overcome these limitations, developers turn to a schema.

A schema describes almost the same structure as the DTD did, but with more detail that's useful for a database, or for another program.

- It's easier to edit, because it is itself written in XML.

- It offers better validation of the content. It does a much better job ensuring that a value is of the right type, and, if necessary, unique.

- It allows easier grouping, substitutions, replacements when we are describing a very large or complicated document type, or when we need to make minor variations for different audiences, product types, purposes.

But writers often find schemas difficult to read.

The DTD may be strange, but once you get the hang of it, you can quickly spot the elements, attributes, and entities that it is defining. As a writer, you can see the pattern fairly quickly.

- A schema is more flexible, appropriate, and useful for database developers and programmers. But it is often more dense and tangled than a DTD, frustrating lay people like us.

- The schema takes up a lot of space. It is what programmers call "verbose." By contrast, the DTD seems sparse and efficient.

- Where a schema is subtle, complex, and sophisticated, a DTD can seem straightforward. The schema begins to resemble object-oriented programming, where the DTD remains closer to a form that writers are familiar with, the outline.

Why not talk more about schemas?

In this book I focus on the Document Type Definition because I have found that easier for writers to understand.

If you can follow the recommendations made in this book, you'll create an XML file that any parser can read.

And, as a writer, you'll find that if you understand how a DTD works with the XML document and stylesheet, you can grasp the very similar relationship with a schema, if you need to take that next step.

What's in the stylesheet?

With an XML document, you can use a cascading stylesheet (CSS) like what you might use with an HTML web page, or you can use a much more complex stylesheet following the standards known as XSLT (the eXtensible Stylesheet Language Transformation).

Both the CSS and XSLT stylesheets describe the format for each element:

- The stylesheet describes the format that the browser should apply to every element, identified by its tag, within the XML document.

  Remember: The XML document is **plain text**. It has no formatting. But it has tags around every piece of content.

- The stylesheet maps to the Document Type Definition, providing a format for every element that the DTD defines.

- As in a book design, the format for each element suggests its purpose, and its relative importance within the "rendered" page.

- As a writer, you do not have to create the stylesheet. Usually, a graphic designer works closely with a programmer to make sure that the browser can "read" and apply these graphic treatments to the contents of the XML document.

- The stylesheet is not a program. It is just a set of rules. The browser does all the work, applying those rules to the elements in the XML document.

The XSLT stylesheet may also perform a lot of transformations (the T in XSLT). When the Parser reads a stylesheet in XSLT, it creates a model of the objects in the document, then uses an XSL processor (another piece of software, usually) to rejigger the contents according to the templates offered by the stylesheet.

An XSLT stylesheet lets you change the actual structure of the document, if you want to. You can reorder, leave out, add, sort, or duplicate particular elements. You can even invoke code.

For example:

- You can move an author's biography to the end of an article.

- You can leave out internal notes, for this version.

- You can sort the product names in a catalog.

59

- You can insert standard text such as a copyright notice, or standard images such as a logo.

- You can include a small script from JavaScript or Python, or refer to a Java class file, or an ActiveX control.

- You can convert XML into HTML, for older browsers.

The part of the stylesheet that carries off these transformations is known as the Transformation. You are transforming one XML document into another, on the fly.

Benefits of transformation:

- One business can use a stylesheet to translate another business's tags.

- You can have a person pick out a particular profile, triggering a particular stylesheet. In effect, you can pick and choose content based on the profile.

- You can make content conditional on a choice, or password.

- You can convert the XML tags into HTML tags so the document looks like a regular HTML page to earlier browsers.

(XSLT can do a lot more than this, but we will leave those aspects for programmers who want to dig into transforming string values, numeric values, dates and times, sequences, sorts, and Boolean values).

What the Parser and the Browser do

1. The Parser analyzes the tagging, and if that is done in the way specified by the version of XML announced in the prolog, the Parser declares the document "well-formed."

2. The Parser compares the structure of the XML document with that described in the Document Type Definition or schema mentioned in the prolog, and if the tags and structures match, the Parser declares the document "valid."

3. The Parser fetches any special characters described in the DTD as "entities," and inserts them into the text in place of the entity references.

4. The Parser replaces the entity references for images, sounds, or videos with the links to those files (using the path or the URL found in the DTD), so that the Browser can insert these items in the page.

5. If the stylesheet is in XSLT, then the Parser and an associated XSL Processor make the changes to the content described in the part of the stylesheet devoted to transformations.

6. The Parser sends the modified file to the Browser.

7. The Browser reads the prolog, and fetches the stylesheet mentioned there.

8. The Browser reads what the stylesheet says about each element (such as "Make it 14 point bold Arial"), looks for that element's start tag, starts formatting the element, and continues that formatting until it reaches the end tag.

9. The Browser repeats this process, formatting elements until it reaches the end of the document.

10. The Browser's rendering engine displays the completely formatted document on the screen.

Exploring the Prolog

A prolog provides five types of information that applications or humans might need to know before reading the document.

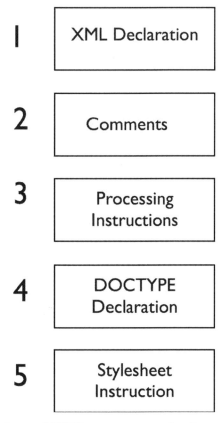

1	XML Declaration
2	Comments
3	Processing Instructions
4	DOCTYPE Declaration
5	Stylesheet Instruction

1a. What version of XML are you using?

The Prolog begins with an XML Declaration. The Parser needs to know what version of XML you are using, to make sure it understands your tags correctly. The most common version these days is 1.0, but there is a version 1.1 and there may be other versions on the way. (Version 1.1 allows new characters in XML names, new line-end conventions, and references to control characters).

1b. What character encoding are you using?

To figure out what characters you mean, the Parser that "reads" or "parses" your document needs to know what set of character codes you are using.

1c. Is there a content model such as a Document Type Definition (DTD) or a schema, and perhaps a related stylesheet, to accompany this document, or does this document stand alone, on its own?

If there is a DTD and stylesheet, the parser will go download those, use the DTD to validate the structure, and apply the transformations from the stylesheet before passing the revised document along to the browser.

2. Do you have any comments for someone else working on this document?

Comments are hidden from the user, but visible to anyone reading the original document.

3. Do you have any processing instructions?

These are direct commands to applications, triggering further processing, or importing some data to place in the document.

4. If you do have a DTD, where is it?

The parser needs the path to the actual Document Type Definition file or schema.

5. If you have a stylesheet, where is it?

The parser and the browser both need the path to the stylesheet file, to download and apply its rules to the document.

To be declared "well-formed" a document does not need a prolog.

An XML parser makes several passes through an XML document. On the first pass, it checks to make sure that the tags have been entered correctly. If so, the parser pronounces the document well-formed. That just means that the markup follows the rules for XML.

Key point: Because the prolog is optional, the parser does not insist on one, when performing this first pass. A document, then, can be judged to be well formed without having a prolog. Of course, you can still have a prolog and be judged well formed; you just don't have to have a prolog, to qualify.

To qualify as well-formed, a document just needs a body, and even within that body, it only needs a single element.

63

Still, it is best practice to include a prolog, no matter what, because it answers so many questions for humans—and software.

If you want your document declared "valid" you must have a prolog.

If you want to have your document validated, by having the parser compare the arrangement of these tags—the structure of this document—with the content model in the Document Type Definition or schema, then you must have a prolog, because that is the place where you tell the parser where the DTD is.

Example of prolog for a valid XML document

```
<?xml version='1.0' encoding='UTF-8'
standalone='no' ?>
<!--File Name: booklist.xml -->
<?calendarapp SELECT date FROM
schedule.cal?>
<!DOCTYPE BookList SYSTEM
"http://www.gobi.org/booklist.dtd">
<?xml-stylesheet type='txt/css'
href='booklist.css'?>
```

XML Declaration	`<?xml version='1.0' encoding='UTF-8' standalone='no' ?>`
Comments	`<!--File Name: booklist.xml -->`
Processing Instructions	`<?calendarapp SELECT date FROM schedule.cal?>`
DOCTYPE Declaration	`<!DOCTYPE BookList SYSTEM "http://www.gobi.org/ booklist.dtd">`
Stylesheet Instruction	`<?xml-stylesheet type='txt/css' href='booklist.css'?>`

64

1. The XML Declaration identifies the XML version, character encoding, and standalone nature of the document.

You start the prolog with an XML declaration. Like all the parts of the prolog, this is optional. But, if you include an XML declaration, you **must** put it at the very beginning of the file, as the first item in the prolog.

<?	XML	Version #	Character encoding	Standalone	?>

1a. Start the file with an opening angle bracket. <

No spaces, line breaks, carriage returns, nothing ahead of the less-than sign, at the very beginning of the file.

The opening angle bracket signals the parser that you are starting some XML markup.

1b. Put a question mark after that.

The question mark signals the parser that you are starting to write an instruction to a program, specifically, the parser.

So these are the first two characters of declaration:

<?

1c. Type: xml

This is a reserved word, meaning that you can't fling it around with abandon because the parser and the XML standard have reserved it for their own use. The parser understands that when you go <?xml you are about to tell it what version of XML you are using.

1d. Type: version='1.0'

If you include the XML declaration, you must include the XML version number. The version is an attribute of XML; that is, the version is one way of describing the type of XML you are using. In this case, the name of the attribute is *version* and the value is usually "1.0." There is a version 1.1, but we are focusing on the more common version in this book. The version attribute is part of the XML declaration because the creators of XML anticipate that there will be many more versions in the future.

65

Note: Put values in straight quotes.

You can use single or double quotes around values, as long as you use the same kind at the beginning and end. (If a value includes one kind of quote, surround it with the other kind of quotes).

Make sure that your quotes are straight, not curly. (Turn off automatic formatting in your word processing tool).

Perfectly good examples of values:

```
<?xml version= '1.0' encoding='UTF-8'
standalone='yes' ?>

<?xml version= "1.0" encoding= "UTF-8"
standalone="yes" ?>
```

Next: If you include **encoding** and **standalone** attributes as parts of the XML declaration, put them in that order, after the version info. (Both optional).

1e. Type: encoding= " followed by the encoding, and close quotes. (Optional attribute)

Include the encoding attribute if you are using special characters, or codes not forming part of the Unicode standards UTF-8 or UTF-16.

- Character code: A number corresponding to a particular character. The standard defines which numbers correspond to which characters.

- Character encoding: The standard way those numbers are expressed (in how many bytes, for instance).

Examples of character encoding

- American Standard Code for Information Interchange (ASCII). 7-bit or 8-bit. Based on the codes used in telegraph signals, which were basically on-off-on-off, to send text messages over wires, the ASCII table is built on bits, the computer equivalent of those on-and-off signals, represented as 1's and 0's. When you have 7 positions for bits, you can create a total of 128 numbers (that is, 2 to the 7th power). These codes go from 0000000 to 1111111, or, in decimal numbers, from 0 to 127. 33 codes refer to nonprinting characters or punctuation; the others refer to letters of the alphabet, symbols such as the dollar sign, or punctuation, such as parentheses. For example, 65 is

66

uppercase A, and 97 is lowercase a. That's ASCII-7. Most computer systems add another bit, to make a byte (eight bits), expanding the range of numbers to go from 0 through 255. Unfortunately, the definitions of those added codes differ from one company to another. And we need even more codes if we want to represent languages such as Chinese or Arabic.

- Unicode Transformation Format-8 (UTF-8) uses one byte for each of the characters in 7-bit ASCIII, and tricks for additional characters. Any pure ASCII text, then, can be thought of as a subset of UTF-8.

- Unicode Transformation Format-16 (UTF-16) assigns two bytes for every character, for 65,356 possible characters, and four bytes for additional characters, for a total of 1,112,064. Most Unicode characters have been organized in blocks such as Extended Latin, Greek, Hebrew, Arabic, Han.

- ISO-8859-1 and Windows-1252 are variations on ASCII, but not subsets of UTF-8.

- Extended Binary Coded Decimal Interchange Code (EBCDIC) is an eight-bit character encoding derived from IBM's work on punched cards back in the 1950's.

If you do not specify an encoding, the parser assumes UTF-8 or UTF-16, and if it encounters something else, fails.

Of course, not every parser recognizes something like the Windows-1252 character set (often spawned by Microsoft applications). If so, try ISO-8859-1, which is similar.

If your document doesn't use any special characters such as accents or weird bullets, use ASCII, or just leave the encoding attribute out, in which case the parser will treat the document as UTF-8. (Usually OK).

Examples of XML declarations with encoding attributes:

```
<?xml version= '1.0'
encoding='windows-1252' standalone=
'yes'?>
<?xml version= '1.0' encoding='UTF-16'
standalone= 'yes'?>
```

> Q: As writers, do we have to know all this encoding stuff?
>
> A: No. You need to understand why it's included, and you need to find out what encoding your software uses, so you can tell the parser. But you will probably not change the encoding very often after that.

1f. Enter the standalone attribute, with a value of yes or no. (Optional attribute).

Announce whether or not this document is a standalone—if you want. This attribute is optional, and some parsers ignore it.

If the parser does not need any other document to understand this XML document, you announce that, yes, this one is a standalone.

Example of standalone document
```
<?xml version= '1.0' encoding='UTF-8'
standalone= 'yes'?>
```

If you have created a Document Type Definition or schema by which the parser can validate this document, then this document is **not** a standalone.

Example of a document that does not stand alone
```
<?xml version= '1.0' encoding='UTF-16'
standalone= 'no'?>
```

1g. Enter a question mark.

1h. End the XML declaration with a closing angle bracket.

Tip: You can press Return between your XML declaration and the next part of the prolog, if you want. The carriage return helps humans read the document. Similarly, you can indent some lines, to distinguish one element from another. XML parsers preserve all white space.

- If you have defined an element to contain "parsed character data" (PCDATA), the parser takes the white space as part of the data.

- If not, it considers the white space "extraneous," and tells the browser so, even while passing the white space along.

Example of a complete XML declaration
```
<?xml version= '1.0' encoding=
'windows-1252' standalone= 'no'?>
```

2. Comments are notes to humans, only.

Use comments for notes to yourself, your team, or some other human being. Once you are inside a comment, you can write any darn thing you want. The XML parser ignores the comments.

You can put comments anywhere you want inside an XML document—in the prolog, body, or epilog.

<!--Comment-->

2a. Start the comment with an angle bracket, an exclamation point, and two hyphens.

This strange set of punctuation alerts the parser that you are starting a comment. Once the parser sees this combination of characters, it ignores everything you write until it reaches two more hyphens and a closing angle bracket.

Tip: Make sure you have turned off the auto-correction that transforms double hyphens into dashes.

Example of starting a comment:

```
<!--
```

2b. Write anything you want.

Caution: Do not try to put a double hyphen inside the comment!

2c. End the comment with two hyphens and an angle bracket.

Examples of complete comments:
```
<!--File Name: booklist.xml-->
<!--This is a first draft for internal
circulation only.-->
<!--Date: July 4, 2021 -->
```

3. Processing Instructions pass commands to software.

If you want to ask an application to run a process, find some data, or do a calculation and return the results, you put the commands into a processing instruction (PI). The parser will pass the command along to the software for action.

Your programming team might hand you a PI to do something like:

- Tell the browser application what stylesheet to use.

- Set up a hook for scripts or server-side inclusions.

- Extend a schema that cannot otherwise be modified.

- Extend a document without changing the DTD.

- Sneak in advice about presentation without altering the structure of the document.

You can put a PI anywhere in the document, except in unparsed character data (CDATA) where it would be mistaken for ordinary text. PI's often go in the prolog.

<? | Target Application | Instruction | ?>

Q: I am not a programmer. How do I know what instructions to give a particular application or applet?

A: You don't. You rely on real programmers to tell you what the processing instructions should say.

3a. Start with a less-than symbol and a question mark.

3b. Include the name of the application that should receive the processing instruction, then give the instruction.

Generally, this information comes from a knowledgeable programmer.

Note: The instructions must not include the closing tag of a question mark followed by the greater-than sign. (That combination is considered the end of the PI by the XML parser).

3c. End with a question mark and a greater-than sign.

Examples of processing instructions:

```
<?xml-stylesheet type='txt/css'
href='booklist.css'?>
<?weatherapp SELECT forecast FROM
National IN nasafeed?>
```

The PI referring the browser to a stylesheet begins with the string **xml**, which is legal only because this particular PI has been blessed by the W3C, in a recommendation.

The second PI tells a calendar application to take the value for forecast from a record called National in a file fed to the system by NASA.

Pause for review

1. What are the three possible parts of an XML document?

2. Which part is required?

3. What is the first character in an XML document?

4. What does encoding refer to?

5. What makes an XML document standalone?

6. What is an XML declaration?

7. What makes an XML document well-formed?

8. What should you surround a value with?

9. What is UTF-8?

10. What syntax indicates that you are writing a comment?

11. What is a processing instruction?

12. What is the general structure of a PI?

Challenges on the first parts of a prolog

0) Write a prolog for a standalone XML document, encoded in UTF-16. Include a comment that this is a draft description of the contents of the standard grocery store, and a comment indicating that the filename is PigglyWiggly.xml. Include a PI asking the calendarapp to select the date from the file schedule.cal.

1) Write a prolog for an XML document with the filename SuperDuper.xml, which does not depend on an external file. Include a comment giving the filename, and another comment saying that this is a draft description of the contents of a standard SuperDuper grocery store. Include a PI asking the calendarapp to select the date from the file schedule.cal.

> Q: How can I find out if my answers are right?
>
> A: Look on the next page for the answers to challenges. Reviews, well, you are on your own with those; you have to look back through the text to find the answers, or reason them out.

Solution to Challenge 0:

```
<?xml version= '1.0' encoding='UTF-16'
standalone= 'yes'?>
<!--File Name: PigglyWiggly.xml -->
<!--This is a draft description of the
contents of our standard grocery
store. -->
<?calendarapp SELECT date FROM
schedule.cal?>
```

Solution to Challenge 1:

```
<?xml version= '1.0' encoding='UTF-16'
standalone= 'yes'?>
<!--File Name: SuperDuper.xml -->
<!--This is a draft description of the
contents of a standard SuperDuper
grocery store.-->
<?calendarapp SELECT date FROM
schedule.cal?>
```

4. The DOCTYPE declaration identifies what type of document this is, so **the** parser can validate its structure.

To let the parser validate the XML document, you place a DOCTYPE declaration within the XML document's prolog. You are telling the parser what kind of document this is, by identifying the Document Type Definition (DTD) or the equivalent schema.

Examples of document types:

- Procedure

- Brochure

- DataSheet

- Concept

The DOCTYPE declaration usually identifies the type of document, and the location of the file that describes its standard structure.

Exceptions: The DOCTYPE declaration may also include the entire DTD— though this is not a great idea, most of the time—or an internal subset of the DTD.

The parser reads the declaration carefully. The DOCTYPE declaration tells the parser the name of the type, and gives the location of its DTD (if in another file), and, possibly, adds a local portion of the DTD, or, in rare cases, offers an entire DTD right within the declaration. One way or another, the declaration gives the parser a way to discover the content model for this document, so it can check the tags and their structure against the ideal form described in the DTD. The parser uses the DTD (from wherever) to validate the document.

To avoid confusing the parser, you can only have one content model for the document; therefore, you may include only one DOCTYPE declaration.

4a. Place the DOCTYPE declaration after the XML declaration, and before any elements.

The declaration must occur before the body of the document—the part that contains the elements with actual content.

In general, we put the declaration right after the XML declaration, but you can put comments and processing instructions between the XML declaration and the DOCTYPE declaration, if you really want to.

The DOCTYPE declaration contains several parts.

- The keyword, DOCTYPE, indicating to the parser that this section says what file contains the definition of this type of document (a DTD or schema), and where that file can be found.

- The name of the element that includes all the content within the document, known as the **document element**, or root element. For example, if you are creating a procedure, the root element would be called *procedure*, on the theory that it includes all the other elements.

- The source, an indication of the general location of the file that contains the Document Type Definition, which can be in a file on your system, or out on the web, in some publicly available site.

- The path to the location of that file, including the name of the DTD file itself, with the possibility of offering a second location.

- (Optionally) an internal DTD, or partial DTD.

The DOCTYPE Declaration, then, has a lot of parts to guide the parser and browser to the file that defines the structure of the document, and its tags.

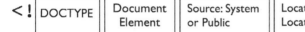

| < ! | DOCTYPE | Document Element | Source: System or Public | Location 1, Location 2 | Internal DTD if any | > |

Example DOCTYPE declaration:

```
<!DOCTYPE product SYSTEM
"http:www.abc.com/product.dtd">
```

Q: There are a lot of D-words in XML, aren't there?

A: Yes, the DOCTYPE declares what the type of document is, and points to the Document Type Definition, a file with the extension .dtd. Is that enough d's for you?

These clusters of words and phrases that sound alike, and mean almost the same thing, can be baffling at first, and even experienced taggers will use the word "description" when they mean "definition." Don't brood about this. You'll get the hang of it.

4b. Start the declaration with XML tag delimiters, the angle bracket (<) and an exclamation point (!).

4c) Add the keyword DOCTYPE.

DOCTYPE is an official XML keyword, and it means Document Type. The idea is that your DTD has defined the logical structure and tags for a particular kind of document. You are about to name that document type, and give directions for finding the file that describes it.

4d) Name the document element (the element that includes the whole content of the document).

The document element, also known as the *root element*, is the top element in the hierarchy defined in your DTD. Usually the name of the DTD is built on this element's name. For instance, if you are making a catalog, you may name your DTD catalog.dtd, and the top element will probably be "catalog." Logically enough, the name you put here in the DOCTYPE declaration would be *catalog*.

Example of the beginning of the DOCTYPE declaration:

```
<!DOCTYPE catalog
```

4e) Identify the type of source (SYSTEM or PUBLIC) and the location(s) of the DTD file.

There are two kinds of **source**.

If you can provide a specific location for the file, you use SYSTEM, on the theory that the file exists on your system, or maybe someone else's system.

In the extremely rare case where you do not know where the DTD is, or it is so common that every parser knows it by heart, or can find it in an instant, you announce that the source is PUBLIC. Oddly, even in this case, you are encouraged to provide a second locator, which is, well, a path leading directly to the file on a particular system.

Best practice: Use SYSTEM.

SYSTEM

If you can provide a specific location, use SYSTEM, and give the Uniform Resource Identifier (consisting of a Uniform Resource Locator or Uniform Resource Name, i.e., URL or URN).

76

Using a URL

Most often you use an ordinary Web address—like this:

1. Start with quotation marks, to introduce the value.

2. Name the protocol scheme (http, mailto, ftp, gopher, news, telnet, file).

3. Add a colon.

4. Give a path to the resource (the rest of the URL).

5. Close with quotation marks at the end.

SYSTEM location using URL

Examples of SYSTEM locations using a URL:

```
<!DOCTYPE Yurtplan SYSTEM
"http://www.gobi.org/yurtplan.dtd">

<!DOCTYPE book SYSTEM
"file:///usr/local/xml/docbook/3.1/doc
book.dtd">
```

Using a Uniform Resource Name (URN)

In rare cases, you may use a URN to describe the system location of the DTD.

The URN is the second flavor of Uniform Resource Identifier. (The first, and most common is the Uniform Resource Locator or URL, the Web address we are familiar with).

The Uniform Resource Name is used to give a unique, location-independent name for a resource such as a standard DTD.

To identify the context of the name of the DTD—where it comes from—we must identify something called a namespace, a metaphysical cloud containing a bunch of specific names all related to a particular category of information (such as names for files, products, or books). In a URN, the namespace might be a company or a standards organization such as the w3.org.

77

1. Begin with quotation marks, to introduce the value.

2. Put in the letters urn, to say what kind of location you are describing.

3. Add a colon.

4. Enter a Namespace Identifier (NID) such as w3.org.

5. Add another colon.

6. Type the unique, and persistent name (the Namespace Specific String, or NSS). That's the actual name of the DTD or schema.

7. Close with quotation marks at the end.

SYSTEM location using URN

Example of a SYSTEM location using a URN
```
<!DOCTYPE FeatureList SYSTEM
''urn:w3.org:xhtml.dtd'' >
```

Q: I barely understand most URLs. Do I really have to learn URIs and URNs?

A: Generally, no. For most situations, the URL is going to be fine.

Why we have namespaces

If you merge two XML documents that happen to use the same element name for two different purposes, you might confuse the parser, and any software that goes searching through your document.

> **Example**:
>
> You start with one document describing a citizen, and that document uses **title** to refer to an honorific such as Reverend or Doctor. Then you add that person's resume, which, unfortunately, uses **title** to describe a job title, as in "Accountant." The parser might declare the document invalid because it expects the first title to be a component in an element called Contact.Info, and choke when a title appears as an element within something called Work.History. And even if

the document were validated, and you were to search for people with the title "Mr.", the results might include items such as "MRP Data Corp" under "Work.History."

To clarify the source of each set of elements, you assign each set to its own namespace, at the start of the document.

To declare that an element belongs to a particular namespace, along with all its children, you insert a shorthand prefix ahead of the element name, followed by a colon, and the name, and an xmlns attribute that identifies that prefix with a unique namespace (usually a URL for an organization).

Namespace Declaration

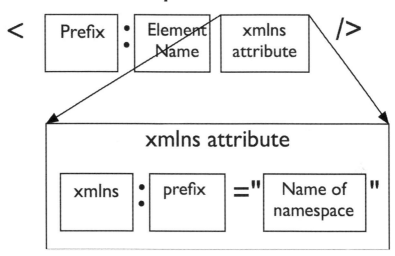

Examples of declaring a namespace
```
<hr:title
xmlns:hr=''http://www.theprices.com/
human.resources''/>

<bk:title
xmlns:hr=''http://www.theprices.com/
book''/>
```

From now on, you would tag the word *President* as "hr:title" to distinguish it from the name of a book such as *The Great Gatsby*, which would be tagged as "bk:title. "

PUBLIC

If you are using a "well-known" industry-standard DTD, which may live on a local server, or be available over a private network, you may use a general, non-specific reference.

The public identifier can be any string of upper or lowercase letters, numbers, plus white space, and apostrophes, parentheses, plus and minus signs, slashes, equal signs, question marks, colons, and commas.

Formal Public Identifier

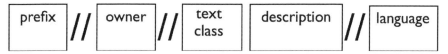

The structure of a public identifier follows the ISO 8879 standard. The prefix is a plus sign (+) if formally registered; but most are a minus sign (-). Text classes include DOCUMENT, DTD, ELEMENTS, ENTITIES.

The DocBook DTD, for instance, is not formally registered; belongs to a group called Oasis; appears in version 3.1, in English.

Example of PUBLIC location:
```
<!DOCTYPE book PUBLIC ''-//OASIS//DTD
DocBookV3.1//EN''>
```

> Q: How often do we have to come up with these public identifiers?
>
> A: Not very often. Generally, the location info is given to you as part of a template. If you have to create the public identifier by yourself, you can copy, paste, and edit to generate any others you need. It's hard coming up with one of these the first time, but after that, you just reuse the identifier over and over.

1. Start the whole Formal Public Identifier with quotation marks.

2. Put in the prefix (usually a minus sign, unless the identifier has been formally registered (almost none have been), followed by slash, slash.

3. Give the owner of the DTD, followed by two slashes.

4. Identify the class of text (usually dtd).

5. Describe the DTD, usually by giving its title or root element, followed by two slashes.

6. Give the code for the language in which the DTD is written.

7. Close the quotation marks.

8. Because that location may be unavailable, or unknown, give a second (SYSTEM) location, that is, a specific path to the file, without bothering to identify this as a SYSTEM location—within its own set of quotes.

- No comma between the two locations.

- Each location gets its own surrounding quotes.

- Although the second location is a SYSTEM location, you do not toss that word into the declaration here. It is implied.

Example of PUBLIC location followed by second location:
```
<!DOCTYPE FeatureList PUBLIC
"ManchuCollaborativeYurt"
"http://www.gobi.org/yurtplan.dtd" >
```

4f) If you are including all of the DTD within the document, put that here within square brackets, instead of the source and location.

Example

Here is an internal DTD within the DOCTYPE declaration, defining a document element called MESSAGE, which may contain any kind of content.
```
<?xml version='1.0' encoding='UTF-8'
standalone='yes'?>
<!DOCTYPE MESSAGE
  [<!ELEMENT MESSAGE ANY>]>
<MESSAGE>Diver below.</MESSAGE>
```

4g) If you are appending an internal subset, put it after the external location.

Your declaration can point in two directions—outward, to an external DTD file, and inward, to some local additions or refinements. You still have one DOCTYPE declaration. It just has two parts—the external subset and the internal subset.

You might want to use the external subset of the DTD for a generic description of this type of document, and the internal subset for:

- Local variations

- Exceptions

- Overrides

- Entities you are only going to use in this particular instance.

Key: The internal subset takes precedence over the external subset.

Example of a DOCTYPE declaration with external and internal subsets.

Here the standard template for the AstroNewsItem lives externally in astronewsitem.dtd, but the internal subset specifies a particular picture for this item.

```
<?xml version='1.0'?>
<!DOCTYPE ASTRONEWSITEM SYSTEM
''file:///site/astronewsitem.dtd'' [
<!ENTITY GAGARIN SYSTEM ''
file:///site/gagarinphoto.jpg'' NDATA
JPG>]>
<ASTRONEWSITEM>
<TITLE>First Human in Space</TITLE>
<DATE>April 12, 1961</DATE>
<NEWS>On this day Yuri Gagarin rode
the Vostok 1 spacecraft to an altitude
of 200 miles above the Earth, to
become the first human in space. He
circled the Earth once. He said,
&quot;The sky is very dark; the Earth
is bluish. Everything is seen very
clearly.&quot;
&GAGARIN;
</NEWS>
</ASTRONEWSITE>
```

Output

First Human in Space

April 12, 1961

On this day Yuri Gagarin rode the Vostok 1 spacecraft to an altitude of 200 miles above the Earth, to become the first human in space. He circled the Earth once. He said, "The sky is very dark; the Earth is bluish. Everything is seen very clearly."

4h. End with a greater-than character.

You have completed your DOCTYPE declaration.

Challenges on DOCTYPE declarations

Challenge 2

Write an XML declaration and then a DOCTYPE declaration for a document element known as Bibliography, referring to that well-known DTD called Bibliography.dtd from the ABIBLIO, the American Bibliography Association. The DTD is also available at http://www.abiblio.org/ templates/bibliography.dtd.

Is the document containing this DOCTYPE declaration standalone or not? (And where would you say so?)

Bonus Question: What is a DOCTYPE declaration, and how does it differ from a Document Type Definition (DTD)?

Challenge 3

Write an XML declaration and then a DOCTYPE declaration for the document element known as Channel, which is described in a well-known DTD promulgated by EG, the Example Society of America, with a copy placed at http://www.example.com/standards/Channel.dtd.

What is the source, here, and what are the locations?

Is the document containing this DOCTYPE declaration standalone or not? (And where would you say so?)

Challenge 4:

In the following XML document, please figure out the location of the DTD, and the purpose of the internal subset of the DTD.

```
<?xml version="1.0" standalone="no"?>
<!DOCTYPE product_features SYSTEM
"http://www.theprices.com/
dtd/product_features.dtd" [
<!ENTITY Jpimage SYSTEM
"http://www.theprices.com/images/Jpimage.jpg
" NDATA JPG>]>
<product_features>
&Jpimage;
Our instant review service gives you
feedback on proposed web pages within 24
hours, so you can get back to work with an
informed, outside critique. We make detailed
recommendations you can act on.
</product_features>
```

Answers

Challenge 2

```
<?xml version="1.0" standalone="no"?>
<!DOCTYPE Bibliography PUBLIC "-
//ABIBLIO//DTD Bibliography//EN"
"http://www.abiblio.org/templates/Bibl
iography.dtd">
```

This is not a standalone document. The source is the actual DTD file; the locations are a public source, at ABIBLIO, and the http address.

The DOCTYPE declaration points to the Document Type Definition, or DTD.

Challenge 3

```
<?xml version="1.0" standalone="no"?>
<!DOCTYPE Channel PUBLIC "-//EG//DTD
Channel//EN"
"http://www.example.com/standards/Chan
nel.dtd">
```

This document is not a standalone. The DTD is Channel.dtd, from the famous EG organization. The file is located on the example.com site.

Challenge 4

The DTD is located at http://www.theprices.com/dtd/product_features.dtd.

The internal subset is used to specify an image to be used in this document, but probably not needed in other documents of this type.

5. A special kind of processing instruction points to the stylesheet, if any.

Stylesheet Instruction

<? | xml-stylesheet | type | = | " Type "

Href | = | " Location " ?>

5a. Put this instruction somewhere after the XML declaration, and before the end of the prolog.

5b. Begin with angle bracket and question mark.

5c. Announce that you are dealing with a stylesheet.

You are talking to the XML parser here, so that is the target application. You are telling the parser to go out and find the stylesheet and bring it back (and apply it, if the document is well-formed and valid).

Example of starting the PI
```
<?xml-stylesheet
```

5d. State the type of stylesheet you are referring to—inside quotation marks.

The file is a text file, and it is probably either a Cascading Stylesheet (css) or eXtensible Stylesheet Language (xsl) document. *Type*, here, is an attribute, and its value must be in quotes. The parser recognizes "text/xsl" as meaning a text file that is written in eXtensible Sylesheet Language.

Example of type
```
<?xml-stylesheet type="text/xsl"
```

5e. Give the location of the stylesheet, and close the PI with a question mark and angle bracket.

86

Example of stylesheet PI with absolute location

```
<?xml-stylesheet type="text/xsl"
href="http://www.theprices.com/
product.xsl"?>
```

You can use a full URL, or if the stylesheet is in the same directory as the XML file, a relative URL.

Example of stylesheet PI with relative location

```
<?xml-stylesheet type="text/xsl"
href="product.xsl"?>
```

Challenge 5

Write the processing instruction to refer the processor to a stylesheet called zippy.xsl at the top level of the domain www.us.gov.

Review of the Prolog

1. What file does the parser use to validate an XML document?

2. What is the difference between a Document Type Definition (DTD) and a DOCTYPE declaration?

3. What is the difference between SYSTEM and PUBLIC locations?

4. Distinguish between a URI, a URL, and a URN.

5. In what circumstances would you need to use namespaces?

6. How do you declare a namespace?

7. Can a DTD occur entirely within an XML document?

8. If a DTD has an external and internal part, which overrides the other?

9. How do you write an internal DTD?

10. What role does a stylesheet play?

Answer to Challenge 5:

```
<?xml-stylesheet type= "text/xsl"
href="http://www.us.gov/zippy.xsl">
```

Questions and Answers about the Prolog

Q: Why have a prolog separate from the body?

To separate information aimed (mostly) at software from the actual content of the document, aimed primarily at people.

Q: How hard is it to learn the rules of XML, the whaddyacall it, the syntax?

A: Learning the rules of XML is a lot easier than learning English grammar. XML was invented by a small team, dedicated to efficiency, consistency, and simplicity, unlike English syntax, which was created by the people, in constant conversation.

Q: Must we have a prolog?

A: No. The only part of an XML document that you must have is the **root element**, which lives at the top level of the Body. Odd fact: None of these sections starts with a tag saying, "Now we start the prolog," or something like that. The parser decides that the prolog has begun when it sees an XML declaration, and that the body has begun when it sees the first element tag, which it assumes identifies the root element, under which all other components live.

XML Declaration

Q: Do we have to have an XML declaration?

A: If you have anything in the prolog, you must start the whole file, and therefore the prolog, with the XML declaration. If you leave this out, of course, the parser will just guess about the version and encoding, and figure that you have no DTD.

Q: If I have an apostrophe within a value, can I surround the value with single quotes?

A: No. The apostrophe is regarded as a single quote. So you would need to surround that value with double quotes.

Q: How many versions of XML are there?

A: Only two so far. The inventors of XML, though, anticipate many more versions, and therefore want to tell the parser which version is being used. Knowing the version lets the parser know exactly what standards the document must meet.

Q: Why encoding?

You've seen documents that have a bunch of rectangles in place of foreign characters. If the parser does not know what kind of characters it is looking at, Arabic, say, or Japanese Hiragana, or French, it may not be able to "read" it well enough to figure out what is going on. Hence, the ugly rectangles. **Encoding** tells the parser how to interpret the characters in the text.

Straight Quotes

Q: Why do we have to use straight quotes in markup?

Within your markup, you must use straight quotes and apostrophes, not curly ones.

Why?

The parser expects them, that's why.

But why?

The codes for straight single and double quotes appear in ASCII, the encoding that every program understands, so these codes survive no matter what encoding you are using. But because the basic ASCII set did not include codes for curly quotes, different systems of encoding use different codes for those characters, so as your text moves from one computer to another, those characters may bomb.

Raymond Chen says:

> Smart quotes—you know, those fancy quotation marks that curl "like this" 'and this' instead of standing up straight "like this" 'and this'—are great for text meant for humans to read. Like serifs and other typographic details, they act as subtle cues that aid in reading.
>
> But don't let a compiler or interpreter see them.
>
> In most programming languages, quotation marks have very specific meanings. They might be used to enclose the text of a string, they might be used to introduce a comment, they might even be a scope resolution operator. But in all cases, the language specification indicates that the role is played by the quotation mark U+0022 or apostrophe U+0027. From the language's point of view, the visually similar characters U+2018, U+2019, and U+02BC (among others) are completely unrelated.
>
> https://blogs.msdn.microsoft.com/oldnewthing/20090225-00/?p=19033

What to do?

In markup, always use straight single and double quotes in pairs.

Q: Can I use curly quotes in my content?

Yes, but... In content, if you want curly quotes, replace them with the codes recognized by all encoding character sets, such as UTF-8.

As David Wheeler says:

> For left and right double quotation marks, use “ and ” and for left and right single quotation marks (and apostrophes), use ‘ and &#8217.
>
> https://www.dwheeler.com/essays/quotes-in-html.html

These codes are **entity references**. What's that mean?

The codes point to entities, that is, specific characters. When the parser encounters one of these codes, it replaces the code with the character, before passing the content to the browser for display.

In that way, the content appears to the viewer with curly quotes.

But in markup, you must always use straight quotes, or else your file will be judged ill-formed and invalid.

Comments

Q: Are comments optional?

A: Of course. So are processing instructions. And if you have a simple document, and no need to have it verified or processed by software, you don't have to include a DOCTYPE declaration, or Stylesheet instruction.

Q: What does the parser do with comments?

A: The parser ignores them, skipping to the punctuation that marks the ending—the two hyphens followed by the closing angle bracket.

DOCTYPE Declaration

Q: Who creates the DTD?

A small team of experts from the groups for technical communication, content management, and database administration get together to hammer out the DTD. The writer explains what the key elements are, what they do for the user, and what they should be named. The other folks write the DTD or schema.

And they test it to make sure it does not break...before you have to use it.

Because it takes a lot of work to set up the DTD and stylesheet, a small team usually does that for the whole group, and you just use what they create. The company begins to see a return on its investment when the writers turn out ten, fifteen, a hundred documents all of the same type…and now, they are all consistently organized and formatted, with re-use of many common elements.

Q: Can we change the DTD later?

Yes, you can expand your DTD at a later date. The important thing will be to make sure you are not trampling on elements that you have already put into fifty documents that use the same DTD. You have to keep those elements alive. Then you can add an OPTIONAL element, and go forward. If you make the new element REQUIRED, and the earlier documents do not have the element, they are no longer valid, and they may not get displayed. So before you launch the new DTD, you have to go back to all of those earlier documents, and add the new element…so they can survive the new DTD.

Q: What exactly does the DTD do?

The DTD does not actually find anything, or do anything. It just sits there.

The software known as the parser looks at the DTD, and then at the XML document, to make sure that the tags in the document match those in the DTD, and, in some cases, the parser works with something called an XSLT processor to do validation, such as checking for a number in the price field. But the level of validation is nowhere near as deep as what you get in a database.

Q: If I put a DTD inside every document, doesn't that work against the general idea of XML, where there is one standard, and every document gets checked against it?

A: Yes. Putting an entire DTD inside each document is crazy. Once in a while, OK. But only in special circumstances. The real breakthrough concept in SGML (and XML) was separating the content model from the individual documents that follow that model, so the parser can verify that all those documents are consistently structured.

Q: Why does the parser take two passes through the document?

If the document is not well formed, why should the parser bother to see if it is valid?

When the team was inventing XML, part of the point was to make it lightweight. That is, the team wanted to make the parser fit onto a mobile phone, which (at that time) had very little memory.

Their solution: Make the parser unforgiving. The first pass can be done very quickly, and mercilessly. If that pass shows that even one start tag is missing an end tag, bang, case closed. No need to check it against the DTD.

The parser that is designed to look at HTML, by contrast, has tons and tons of remediation: If someone forgets to go back to a paragraph after doing a heading, the parser says, well, this person probably meant for the heading to end here, and the paragraph to start after that, so we will just make a little correction, for the sake of the stylesheet and browser.

Hence, HTML parsers are enormous.

Nowadays, any smartphone can handle the big parsers...and the little ones. But the habit of making two passes remains, and the tendency to reject anything that does not seem well formed or valid also persists.

Q: How important are namespaces, anyway?

A: The more complex your site, the more often you will have to deal with namespaces. As DTDs multiply, and documents get merged with other documents, you need a way to distinguish tags deriving from one DTD and tags deriving from another. If you are fortunate enough to be working on a fairly simple site, you may only need to recognize the peculiar namespace markup when it shows up in an incoming XML document you must read and analyze.

Stylesheet PI

Q: Do we have to point to a stylesheet?

A: No. But the more documents you turn out, the more you will need stylesheets to keep formatting consistent. If you use content management software, it can swap stylesheets, too, assigning one to a document going to a handheld device, and another for the same document headed for a desktop computer.

What you do with all this stuff

Q: Does the parser help me do debugging?

The parser is not interested in debugging. An XML editor would quickly point out the error. But the parser just says, oops, I am quitting right here. (That's one of the ways that the XML parser stays so lightweight; it has no remediation built in, the way the HTML parser does.) For debugging, then, look to other tools.

Q: How do I pick out the right parser?

As a writer, you do not get to pick what parser the user will have. The user's browser comes with its own parser.

And once it sees that the document is in XML, the browser assigns its own XML parser to review the document. The XML parser is much faster than the one used for HTML, because the XML parser is very small. Why? Because it just follows the rules, with no exceptions.

The HTML parser will forgive almost any error in tagging...and make your page look all right...and that takes a lot of code...so, in nanoseconds, the HTML parser takes longer to complete its tasks.

But, as I say, you are not the one who gets to pick the parser.

Q: Do I have to format all this material by hand?

No. If you have ever written HTML by hand, you know how easy it is to insert two-pixel variations by mistake, or accidental changes in heading formats, from one page to the next, resulting in a slightly uneven effect. Using a stylesheet ensures that all pages look alike...a subtle message that your organization knows what it is doing, and isn't just winging it.

Q: Do I have to enter all these tags by hand?

Good news: You rarely have to do tagging by hand. Usually, you use an XML editor. You tell it, OK, now I am going to do a title, and the editor inserts a start tag before what you write, and after it. You may never see the tags. If you are writing in the view known as WHAT YOU SEE IS WHAT YOU GET, you just see it magically formatted, according to the stylesheet. No hands!

But if you choose the tag view, voilá, the start tag is there in front of what you wrote, and the end tag is after it.

In an XML editor, huzzah, you DO get to see what your text will look like, because the software applies the stylesheet's formatting to each element as you write.

You can then choose to view the tags...if you want...or if you suspect something is going wrong. But many people just write in the WHAT YOU SEE IS WHAT YOU GET view, most of the time. The editor prompts them, saying, OK, here are the elements you can legitimately put into this document at this position. And if you try something different, it beeps at you.

You can turn off the validation, and just write like crazy for a while, and then turn validation back on, when you feel more analytical.

The Body

Remember the goals of XML? In the Body of the XML document, we'll see how the creators of XML built artifacts to meet some of those goals.

Goal: Make all documents of the same type follow the same structure.

To define that structure, we must be able to separate one component from another. And we must be able to tell which is which.

Elements stand out from other parts of the document.

- Each element has a **name**, telling us what it is.

- Each element has a clear **beginning** (indicated by a start tag containing the name) and a clear **ending** (with an end tag).

- Each element can be isolated from other elements because it has carefully marked **boundaries**. (It is enclosed within the start and end tags).

And the DTD or schema spells out the standard way to organize these individual components. It creates a **content model** showing:

- The **names** of every element, indicating what kind of content each one should contain

- The **metadata** describing each element (such as date of creation)

- The standard **sequence** of elements, required or optional

- The elements that **contain** other elements, and the elements that contain nothing but text, or a pointer to some image in another file

- A complete **hierarchy** of all the elements, from top to bottom

When we work in the body of a new document of this type, our XML editor reads the DTD or schema, and nudges us to follow the right sequence and hierarchy, from one element to the next.

Goal: The standard structure should reflect the needs of the users.

In effect, each element should answer one type of **question** from the users. For example, if the users are almost always asking, "How much does it cost?" we create an element called PRICE to answer that question.

- Each element has its own job: To answer one type of user question, to contain only that kind of information.

- Each element contains the actual **content** that the user wants to see.

Goal: Let users find one particular chunk of information.

Instead of offering users an entire document as the result of a browse path or search, we want to be able to give them one particular element.

In advanced search, we can allow users to filter their search by:

- The names of elements

- The actual content inside those elements

- The metadata *about* the elements, such as author, date created, natural language, product category.

To carry the metadata, or information about an element, the team lets us describe the element in **attributes**.

These are not seen by the ordinary user. But on the content team, we can use the attribute values to find elements that we want to reuse (find me all task topics I wrote in June of this year), and the search engine can use the attribute information to refine or filter the results for the user (only show me task topics in French, written in the last year).

Attributes also let us **customize**. In the attribute, out of sight of the users, we can identify some topics as FOR_MANAGERS, and others FOR_GEEKS. Then, when we have a profile of a user as a manager or a geek, we can filter the search results to show only the ones relevant to that group.

Goal: Make sure that the document can be read by anyone's parser and browser.

To make sure that the document can be read by any program, the designers of SGML and XML decided that the document must be created in plain text, without any proprietary formatting or codes.

But that means that the document cannot contain any pictures. And if your raw text is just basic ASCII text, it cannot contain symbols and "foreign" characters.

So the designers invented **entity references**.

In the DTD, an entity reference may:

- Provide the path to a file containing a picture that you want inserted into the document when it is displayed in a browser.

- Identify the standard number for a symbol or foreign character that the parser should fetch and put into the document before passing it to the browser.

Goal: Separate content from structure and format

The key idea behind SGML and XML was to separate these three aspects of a document. But the XML document has to point to the DTD or schema that describes the structure and tags, and to the stylesheet that tells the browser how to format the content.

That's the key job of the Prolog. But the ordinary user never sees the Prolog.

Who gets to see what?

The audience never sees the **prolog**.

The prolog has two users—you and the software.

- As a member of the content team, **you** get to look under the hood, and tweak what the prolog is saying.

- But **software** is the most important user of the prolog—the parser and the browser follow its directions, fetching the information about the standard **structure**, transforming the document, bringing in images, **formatting** the text, and displaying the "rendered" page on the screen, so your users can read the **content**.

But where is the content?

Content is the meaningful information that your audience wants to **see**. That lives in the **body** of the document.

But in the XML document, that content does not appear as it will on the finished page. It is surrounded with tags, enmeshed in strange punctuation, interspersed with comments meant only for the content team, and expanded with processing instructions that bring in live feeds. Software transforms the body into content that the audience can see and interact with.

What the user sees emerges from five components of the Body, identified by markup:

- **Elements**: The building blocks of structure, designed to contain different categories of information in the form of text content, pointers to non-textual content (entity references), and, yes, other elements (such as a serial number element inside a product element).

- **Attributes** of an element: Characteristics or properties of an element, unseen by the audience, but used by the content management system and the search engine.

- **Entity references**: Pointers to "things" such as boilerplate text stored in a central location (for example, standard legal warnings), strange foreign symbols or characters (stored in lists on other servers), images, audio, and video (non-text content that must be fetched from another location and inserted into the page by the parser or browser).

- **Processing instructions**: Commands sent to programs to bring in content such as stock prices, or a weather feed.

- **CDATA sections**: Blocks of "character data," that is, text; but the parser does not examine this text; it just leaves it as is, without looking inside the block. (Rarely used, but occasionally useful).

Elements are key.

An element offers a chunk of content, or points to some content.

Its name describes a **class**: a category of information, such as Destination_City. That's the kind of content that should appear in every particular **instance** of the element, such as Honolulu, Wailuku, or Lahaina.

An element may **contain**:

- A word, such as "Discount."

- A number, such as the serial number for a product.

- A lot of text, such as a complete product description.

- One or more other elements. For example, Destination_City could contain elements such as Destination_City_Outdoor_Fun, and Destination_City_Nightlife.

- Nothing but a pointer to an image, such as the corporate logo.

An element may **be contained** in another element. For example, Destination_City could nest inside of a larger element called Destination.

How can we keep all these elements organized?

The DTD or schema spells out:

- The name of each element (the name used in the start and end tags that surround the actual content, such as <product> and </product>)

- Whether it is required or optional, and when

- What its properties should be (metadata about the content of the element)

- How many instances of the element are required or allowed

- What it must or may contain (its contents)

- What elements it is contained in

- Where it fits within a sequence of elements

Example:

The DTD for Destination could define the element Destination_City in this way:

- It is contained inside of the element Destination.

- It is required.

- Each Destination element must contain one instance of the Destination_City element, but may contain many instances of the Destination_City element.

- The Destination_City element must contain all of the following elements, in this sequence: Destination_City_Description, Destination_City_Weather, Destination_City_Outdoor_Fun, Destination_City_Nightlife, Destination_City_Family_Events, Destination_City_Hotels, Destination_City_Restaurants.

- The metadata for the Destination_City element must include the name of the author, the date of last modification, the natural language, and codes for the related tour packages.

Then the DTD or schema would define all those other elements, one by one.

And it would define the elements that must be contained in the Destination element, in addition to Destination_City, such as Photo_Album, Airfare, Cruises, Destination_Beaches, and Destination_Tours.

Looking at the tree

This abstract description of the content and its organization represents the document as a hierarchy of elements. At the top is the document. Within that we see elements nested within elements, going down, down, down in the structure. At the bottom are the smallest bits of information, such as the Serial_Number or ZIP code.

This tree structure starts with a single item at the top. You might think that the top of the tree would be a leaf, or a branch. But the engineers who designed XML were more poetic than that. They called that top element the root.

So the tree is upside down. The root element is at the top; it is the one that names the document type; it is also known as the document element.

Everything else in the body lives inside of it, grows out of it. So as we explore, moving through the branches and twigs, we end up at the leaves—that is, the smallest possible elements, which usually contain just some piece of raw text, like a brand name.

These leaves are sometimes called nodes, like the devices on a network.

And, because this is a hierarchy, and one element may contain other elements, the container is sometimes called a parent, and the elements that contains are thought of as the children.

Forgive the engineers for their poesy.

The body begins with the root element.

As soon as you see a root element, you know that you have entered the body of the document.

The name of the root element describes the main subject of the document. That's why it is often called "the document element." The Document Type Definition or schema for this type of document usually bears this name. For example, in a document about a process, the root element might be Process, and the DTD would be named process.dtd.

Example of a root element

A document describing a product includes elements for the product number, product names, description, retail price, vendor name, and vendor shelf-keeping unit number (SKU). Those elements all appear as components of a larger element, Product. They are its children. And Product is the root element for the document.

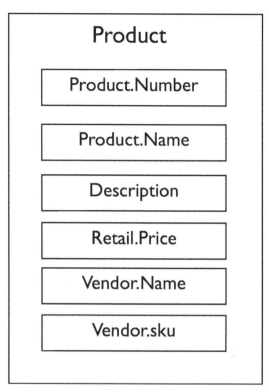

Example of elements nested within Product element

```
<Product>
<Product.Number>51</Product.Number>
<Product.Name>CyberGotcha</Product.Nam
e>
<Description>A fantastic way to
communicate with all your classmates,
without the teacher knowing. Creates
its own cell network within 750 feet.
Send messages, images, sounds, even
video to anyone else with a
CyberGotcha.</Description>
<Retail.Price>$95.95</Retail.Price>
<Vendor.Name>Cyberama</Vendor.Name>
<Vendor.sku>67-90-55a</Vendor.sku>
</Product>
```

Another Example: Booklist is the root element

In a document modeled on the DTD called booklist.dtd, the root element would normally be called *booklist*, and the root element would begin with the tag <booklist>.

```
<booklist>
  <book>
      <title>The Best of Online
      Shopping</title>
      <author>Lisa and Jonathan
      Price</author>
      <pages>500</pages>
      <price>$16.00</price>
  </book>
</booklist>
```

Nesting elements properly

To avoid confusing the parser, XML insists that you follow some rules about organizing your elements.

Rule: If an element starts inside another element, it must end **within** that same element.

```
┌──────────────────────────────┐
│   BookID start tag            │
└──────────────────────────────┘
      ┌──────────────────────────┐
      │   ISBN13 start tag        │
      └──────────────────────────┘
      ┌──────────────────────────┐
      │   ISBN13 content          │
      └──────────────────────────┘
      ┌──────────────────────────┐
      │   ISBN13 end tag          │
      └──────────────────────────┘
┌──────────────────────────────┐
│   BookID end tag              │
└──────────────────────────────┘
```

Rule: If one element follows another, you must end the first before starting the next.

```
┌────────────────────────────┐
│   Star.Name start tag      │
└────────────────────────────┘
         ┌────────────────────────────┐
         │   Star.Name content        │
         └────────────────────────────┘
┌────────────────────────────┐
│   Star.Name end tag        │
└────────────────────────────┘


┌────────────────────────────┐
│   Meteor.Name start tag    │
└────────────────────────────┘
         ┌────────────────────────────┐
         │   Meteor.Name content      │
         └────────────────────────────┘
┌────────────────────────────┐
│   Meteor.Name end tag      │
└────────────────────────────┘
```

If the XML parser encounters an improperly nested tag, it reports that the document is "not well formed," and quits processing, refusing to display anything (not even the portions of the document that passed muster)—or it just shows the raw text of the XML document.

(In a similar situation, the parser for an HTML browser continues processing, and does its best to figure out what you meant. That's why HTML browsers are so hard to write, and so big. XML is lightweight because its parsers insist you follow the rules.)

Bad examples: Improperly nested elements

```
<product>
<Product.Number>51</product>
</Product.Number>

<park>
<Park.name>Central</park>
<Park.type>Recreation</Park.name></Par
k.type>
```

Properly nested:
```
<product>
<Product.Number>51</Product.Number>
</product>

<park>
<Park.name>Central</Park.name>
<Park.type>Recreation</Park.type>
</park>
```

Challenges

Challenge on a product

Using our Product hierarchy, write the XML for product # 900A, named Gizmo Supreme, described as "The best all-purpose slicer-and-dicer on late-night TV." The retail price is $29.95. The vendor is schlock.ru, and their SKU is 004455.

Challenge on another product

Using our Product hierarchy, write the XML for product # 899, named LowPoint, described as "The tonic to remove unhappy wrinkles." The retail price is $29.95. The vendor is schlock.ru, and their SKU is 009988.

Answers

First challenge on a product

```
<Product>
<Product.Number>900A</Product.Number>
<Product.Name>Gizmo Supreme
</Product.Name>
<Description>The best all-purpose
slicer-and-dicer on late-night
TV.</Description>
<Retail.Price>$29.95</Retail.Price>
<Vendor.Name>schlock.ru</Vendor.Name)
<Vendor.sku>004455</Vendor.sku>
</Product>
```

Second challenge on a product

```
<Product>
<Product.Number>899</Product.Number>
<Product.Name>LowPoint</Product.Name>
<Description>The tonic to remove
unhappy wrinkles.</Description>
<Retail.Price>$29.95</Retail.Price>
<Vendor.Name>schlock.ru</Vendor.Name)
<Vendor.sku>009988</Vendor.sku>
</Product>
```

Attributes

An attribute describes an element. Examples:

- Creator (of the element)
- Date_Modified
- Natural_Language
- Product_Category
- Vendor

The audience does not see the attributes of an element. We do.

- As writers we use these descriptions to find and reuse content. (Fetch the topics I wrote in June, in the category of Perfume).

- The search mechanism uses these descriptions to pick out elements that match a particular criterion, such as "All products from this vendor."

- The content management system uses these descriptions to take actions such as archiving a topic, if none of its elements has been modified in the last year.

Each attribute is made up of two parts: a name, and a value.

- The **name** never changes.

- The **value** changes with the circumstances, and the nature of the element itself. For instance, we always have a Product_Category attribute for every Product, but the value of the attribute may change from Lotion to Perfume to Scrub.

An attribute appears inside the start tag for the element.

Example:

> You have a list of songs, and for each song you say what language it is in. Thus, you have an element called **song**, and an attribute called **language**. For the song "Amie," the value of the language attribute would be FR, for French.

All of that information about the element appears inside the start tag for the element, **song**. The actual content of the element is the name of the song, "Amie."

Start Tag

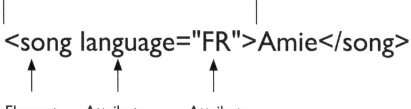

Element Name | Attribute Name | Attribute Value

Tip: Be careful to distinguish the name of the **element** from the name of the **attribute**.

One element may have zero, one, or many attributes. But an element may have only one instance of each attribute.

Comparison

In a way, an element is like a record in a database. In this analogy, the attributes are like the fields on the record, and the attribute values are the values in those fields. In fact, this similarity is part of the reason that programmers can easily move information back and forth between an XML document and a database.

Because attributes are used by the search mechanism and the databases that store the information, the DTD or schema carefully defines what kind of information you can use as a value.

For example:

- You can spell out a list of acceptable values, and refuse to allow any others.

- You can set up an ID attribute for one element, and then link to that ID from elsewhere in the document.

- You can define the value as starting with a number, or a letter, or anything at all.

- You can have the value be something called an entity reference. (In the DTD or schema, you define a code, saying that when the parser sees this code, it should go fetch a file or character at a particular location on the server or on the web).

- You can say that the values must only be the shorthand for certain file types, such as jpg and gif.

107

These criteria are known as data types. They are nowhere near as strict as the data typing that you see in a database. (In a database, for example, you can insist that the user enter a real date in the right format).

And you can make an attribute **required** or **optional**. And, just to be special, the DTD can say, "Well, if you use this optional attribute, you must use this value, and only this value." It's **fixed**.

In general, though, you do not need to worry too much about creating most attributes. You are going to be using an XML editor that follows the DTD or schema, and inserts the attributes as needed, asking you for any input. But you may need to be able to figure out the attributes when reading someone else's XML document.

When is something an element, and when is it an attribute?

Sometimes your team debates a metaphysical issue like this. For example, you could have a long argument over this question: Should Gender be an element nested inside the Employee element, or should Gender be an attribute of the Employee element?

Here's what those alternatives would look like.

Using an Element for gender within Employee

```
<Employee>
   <gender>female</gender>
   <firstname>Camille</firstname>
   <lastname>Doncieux</lastname>
</Employee>
```

Using an Attribute for the gender of an Employee:

```
<Employee gender="female">
   <firstname>Camille</firstname>
   <lastname>Doncieux</lastname>
</Employee>
```

To decide, you have to ask yourself: Do we want to show this information to the user or not?

If you want the user to see the content, it is an element. If you do not want the user to see the value, it is an attribute.

That's a common rule of thumb. Yes, there are exceptions. But it helps to realize that the user never sees the attribute or its value.

Another deciding factor: Because you can only have one instance of an attribute per element, you may need to go to a series of child elements if there are multiple values. For example, if you want to list all of a person's occupations, you might want to display those, and you could say that the Person element may contain one or more instances of the Profession element.

The key, then, is: Who gets to see the information?

Entity References

An entity is a thing that lives outside of the XML document.

You recall that an XML document is just text. So if you want to have the company logo in your document, you need to tell the parser and browser where to find the logo file.

1. In your DTD or schema you put the URL or path to the file, and you create a shorthand term, called an **entity reference**, to stand for that path.

2. You put that entity reference into your XML document.

3. Later the parser replaces the shorthand term with the actual path, and passes the expanded text along to the browser, so that the browser can go out and fetch the logo.

In your XML document, the text appears in some limited set of characters, such as those defined in the standards known as Universal Coded Character Set + Transformation Format—8-bit (UTF-8) or UTF-16. (Basically, that's what we think of as raw ASCII text).

So, if you want to use a symbol or foreign-language character that is not in that set, you need to point to its number in some other character set. The odd symbol or foreign character is an **entity**.

1. In the DTD you create a path to the exact number of that character in the other character set, and create a shorthand term for that path.

2. Then, you insert that "entity reference" into your text, pointing to the character.

3. The parser reads the entity reference in the XML document, looks it up in the DTD or schema, fetches the character, and inserts it into the text, then passes that along to the browser.

And if you want to use one of the characters that are "reserved" for XML's own use, such as the larger-than symbol, you use an entity reference, so that the parser can insert the right character into the text before passing it along to the browser. (You do not need to define these in your DTD because the parser already knows them).

In your document, then, you point to one of those entities by using an entity reference.

Processing Instructions

We've looked at these before. They tell the browser what application to open, and what commands to give that application, so that it can bring back some content to add to the page.

CDATA Sections

These are the "Get out of jail free" cards of XML. The CDATA section escapes inspection by the parser. The parser just skips over one of these sections the way it would ignore a comment.

So you can use a CDATA section for text that you want undisturbed by the parser, or text that has so many reserved characters that it would be tedious to insert all the entity references.

So, yes, a CDATA section is cheating. Officially, the term means "character data," but that does not distinguish this section from the rest of the XML document, which is just text. But the secret meaning is: CHEATING DATA.

Marking up the Body

We've seen that the Body may contain five components that carry or affect the content that the user sees.

- Elements
- Attributes
- Entity references
- Processing instructions
- CDATA sections

Now we will explore the ways we mark up these components.

6. An element offers content labeled by markup.

In an element, content is surrounded by a start tag and an end tag.

- Every tag begins and ends with angle brackets—the less-than symbol, and the greater-than symbol.

- A slash after an opening angle bracket indicates an **end tag**.

- The element name in the start tag and the element name in the end tag must match exactly, including the case of each letter.

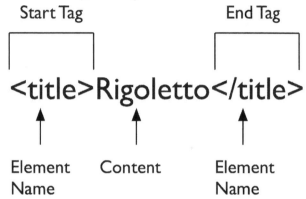

6a. Begin the start tag with an angle bracket.

Use a less-than symbol.

6b. Begin the name of the element with a letter or underscore.

You must start with a letter (including non-Latin characters) or underscore right after the angle bracket.

(No space before the name in the start tag).

And you cannot start off with the letters x, m, and l, in that order, because XML is a "reserved" word. Basically, you do not want to confuse the parser by invoking the deity XML.

Examples of legitimate ways to start a name:

<_shop>

<shop>

<SHOP>

Examples of bad starts:

<99flavor>

<...flavor>

<!flavor>

<xmlflavor>

6c. Type the rest of the element name, which may include zero or more letters, numbers, periods, hyphens, or underscores.

As you type the name, you need to watch your capitalization and spelling, to make sure the element name matches what was defined in the Document Type Definition. If you change one letter, or switch capitalization, the parser will not recognize this as a valid element. (Later, when you write the end tag, you will need to double-check that it matches, too).

OK as part of an element name (after the first character):

- Letters
- Numbers
- Periods
- Hyphens
- Underscores

No-No's

- Do not start an element name with XML in any form: uppercase, lowercase, or mixed. (That's reserved for XML's own use).

- Do not include a space character in an element name.

- Do not include a colon, except right after a namespace you have already declared. (Namespaces help you distinguish elements that have the same name, but come from different sources. For instance, xsl:template describes the element called template in the namespace devoted to the eXtensible Stylesheet Language.)

- Do not use any other punctuation. For instance, you must not use a slash, equal sign, exclamation point, or a bracket, because these could confuse the parser. When writing an element name, just steer clear of all punctuation other than the period, hyphen, or underscore.

Examples of legitimate names:

<Part>

<_3rdPlace>

<A>

<B-ROW>

<street.address.1>

Examples of illegal names:

<2ndplace>

<B Row>

<B/Row>

<:Chapter>

<<coauthor>

< author>

<!key>

<*note>

<Medical#>

<customer/client>

6d. Complete the start tag with a closing angle bracket (the greater-than symbol).

The element name is now surrounded with angle brackets, which set it off, or delimit it. The less-than and greater-than symbols are **delimiters**.

Challenge on element names

Circle any legitimate names, and correct the others:

      <5thElement>

      <_Latin>

      <xmlIdeas>

      < Date>

      <A/Level>

      <calc::result>

      <rule 1>

      <retail price>

      <inventory.item>

      <name-first>

      <!result>

      <2ndprize>

      < order/invoice #>

      <result<0>

      <XML.tag>

      <street-address-1>

      <street.address.2>

      <input::form>

      <lastname>

      <_tree>

Answers

<FifthElement>, ok, <Ideas>, <Date>, <ALevel>, <calcresult>, <rule1>, <retailprice>, ok, ok.

<result>,<secondprize>,<order.inv.number>, <resultzero>, <mytag>, ok, ok, <input.form>, ok, ok.

6e. Enter your content.

Content can contain almost anything. Content within the element can be:

• Nothing at all (legitimate, though rare, for elements where the content is optional)

```
<middle_name></middle_Name>
```

• Parsed character data (ordinary text that will be read by the parser)

```
<firstname>Jonathan</firstname>
```

• Nested elements

```
<book>
   <title>The Best Thing on TV</title>
   <author>Jonathan Price</author>
</book>
```

• Entity references (such as the ones beginning with an ampersand and ending with a semicolon, here, pointing to a product description, and the ampersand character itself)

```
<product>
   Product: &product;
   Partners: Posh &amp; Luxury
</product>
```

• CDATA sections (text that will be left as is, without any parsing)

```
<archive>
<author>Marcel J. Proust</author>
<![CDATA[Use an escape character for
<, OK? ]]
</archive>
```

• Comments (text that is not shown to the user)

```
<review>
<!--Review is still to come.-->
</review>
```

• Processing instructions (commands given to a program or applet)

```
<contact.rating>
The rating is <?MsAccess
Rate=''value'' ?>
</contact.rating>
```

6f. After the content, close the element with an end tag—the less-than symbol, a slash, the element name, and greater-than symbol.

115

End Tag

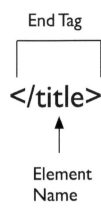

</title>

Element
Name

Unlike HTML, XML insists that you always show where an element stops, by using an end tag.

HTML allows you to leave out the closing tag for a paragraph, and the browsers' parsers are built to figure out when you start a new paragraph.

XML parsers are much lighter, and do not contain any code for figuring out what you meant. You either put the end tag in, or you suffer a blank screen, when the parser condemns your document as ill-formed, and refuses to display anything, not even an error message. (Or it shows the raw text of your XML document itself).

Example of HTML, which lets you omit some end tags.

```
<HTML>
<BODY>
<P>Our customer service is here to make
your online shopping experience
convenient, easy, and incredibly
enjoyable. <BR>We want to help you with
any questions you have. Our mission is
to ensure that your shopping experience
is the best on the Web.
<P>Our store has been created with
your shopping convenience in mind. We
provide a "one-stop" shopping center,
where you have easy access to retail
merchants/stores, auctions, and
classifieds, all in one place.
</BODY>
</html>
```

116

Examples: Bad XML matches between start and end tags:

```
<title>Hamlet</TITLE>
<FIRSTNAME>George</firstname>
<Title>De Rerum Natura</title>
```

Special case: An empty element

Sometimes an element has no content. Or that content is optional.

If the element has no text content, and does not point to another file, you can indicate that the element is "empty" by adding a slash at the end of the start tag, and dropping any end tag. The result is a mishmash that starts and stops at the same time.

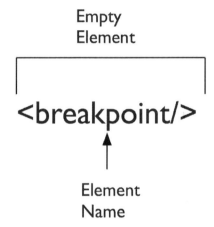

Empty
Element

\

Element
Name

Empty elements like this help you indicate a location within the document, a spot where you want the processing application to take an action. Software can find the spot, but the user sees nothing there, because the empty element contains no text.

In an XML document, the only visible content is text. So what do we do about other stuff?

We add an attribute to the empty element.

Within the document, we can use an attribute in an empty element to point to an image, video, sound clip, strange symbol or logo—any non-text content that exists outside of the actual XML document.

For example, you might have an element called **image** with an attribute called **source**, pointing to an entity called **&logo;**, which is defined in the Document Type Definition with the path to the logo file.

<image source="&logo;"/>

Alternative: You can also just show the start tag, followed directly by the end tag, if the Document Type Definition declared that the element did not need content. Technically, this is different from a pure "empty element."

Review on elements

1. What is a root element?

2. What is a document element?

3. What may be contained within the root element?

4. What tags surround the content of an element?

5. What must an element name begin with?

6. What other characters are allowed in the name, after the first character?

7. Why do you imagine that XML reserves characters such as the less-than sign, refusing to let you include them in an element name?

8, What might you use an empty element for?

9. Why do you think that XML insists on having an end tag for every start tag?

10, What can an element contain?

7. An attribute describes an element.

An attribute is a characteristic of the element.

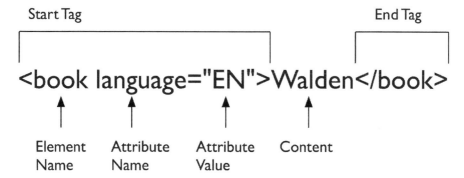

You place an attribute right after the name of the element in the element's start tag, or in an empty element tag.

An attribute has two parts—a name, and a value (which appears in quotes). Or, as a programmer might say, an attribute specification is a name-value pair associated with the element. The name is generic, a category of information. The value, though, is specific to this particular element.

So an attribute has only one name, but it may have different values when it appears in different instances of the element.

An element may have zero, one, or several attributes, separated by spaces. But any particular attribute may appear only once per element (or empty element).

Tip: Within the start tag for an element, if you have several attributes, they may appear in any order, separated by space characters, but for humans, you should probably use a consistent order.

7a. In the start tag (or empty tag), right after the name of the element, put a space, then the name of the attribute.

The name of an attribute resembles the name of a field in a form; the value you type into that field may be different from one element to another, but the name of the attribute remains the same, throughout.

The attribute name begins with a letter or an underscore. After that, you can have zero or more letters, numbers, periods, hyphens, or underscores.

Examples of attributes in start tags:
```
<product sku="e15">
<price type="retail">
<company relationship="vendor">
```

Example of attributes in empty elements:
```
<image file="&logo;"/>
<breakpoint purpose="section.break"/>
<video rating="PG"/>
```

7b. Type an equal sign.

7c. Put in a value (or values) surrounded by two double quotes, or two apostrophes—straight, not curly.

The value applies to this particular instance of the element. The attribute name, then, applies generally to all elements of this type, but the values may differ from one particular instance of that element to another. For example, if the element was Book, you might have an attribute Media, with acceptable values such as Hardbound, Paper, PDF, and eBook.

If you start with an apostrophe, you must end with an apostrophe. If you start with a double quote, end with a double quote. Make sure both are straight, not curly.

Caution: Never put a less-than character into the value.

Caution: Do not put an ampersand into the value except to start a character or entity reference.

Caution: Do not create a value containing the same quote character you are using to delimit the value.

Some elements with attributes and well-quoted values:
```
<price type="retail">$19.95</price>
<title cover="hard"
category="computer">Blown to Bits
</title>
<DVD serial="A56B41" region="B5">
<film>Red Dragon</film>
<vendor>Sony</vendor>
</DVD>
```

Not-so-good attributes

```
<price type="retail">$19.95</price>
<title cover="hard" category=
'computer">Blown to Bits </title>
<DVD serial='A5"6B41" region='5&6">
<film>Red Dragon</film>
<vendor>Sony</vendor> </DVD>
```

Challenges on attributes

Employee Gus Tabut

Create an element called Employee with attributes for status (current), level (G2), and department (Accounting), as well as component elements for First Name (Gus), Last Name (Tabut), Phone Extension (x65), and Email Address (gus.tabut@example.com).

Employee Aloysius Hassenpfeffer

Create an element called Employee with attributes for status (retired), level (G6), and department (Factory), as well as component elements for First Name (Aloysius), Last Name (Has), Phone Extension (x78), and Email Address (has43@example.com).

Answers

Employee Gus Tabut

```
<Employee status="current" level="G2"
department="Accounting">
<First.Name>Gus</First.Name>
<Last.Name>Tabut</Last.Name>
<Phone.Extension>x65</Phone.Extension>
<Email>gus.tabut@example.com</Email>
</Employee>
```

Employee Aloysius Hassenpfeffer

```
<Employee status="retired" level="G6"
department="Factory">
<First.Name>Aloysius</First.Name>
<Last.Name>Has</Last.Name>
<Phone.Extension>x78</Phone.Extension>
<Email>has43@example.com</Email>
</Employee>
```

7d. In writing the value, follow the data type.

For any attribute, the value must be a certain kind of information, such as text or numbers. The DTD or schema tells you what type of data is valid.

In this context, you might think of the attribute name as a kind of question. The answer is the value. But only certain kinds of answers are acceptable. They must be of the right data type.

Example

In the Product element, the attribute is named Pricing. This attribute is asking you "What kind of pricing do you want to apply to this product? Should it be Retail, Wholesale, Special, or Discount?"

Those values are spelled out in the DTD, which says that no other values would be valid. Why not allow some other value, such as Outrageous?

Because the type of data that is acceptable for this particular attribute is "enumerated," that is, already listed in the DTD. Its data type is "enumerated list." That means that any value **not** listed in the DTD is invalid.

A data type sets some kind of criterion for the value.

The DTD or schema describes the criterion. The parser then checks to make sure that the value meets this criterion. (If not, the parser declares the document "invalid.")

In a DTD, there are 10 different data types. In a schema, there are even more, but for our purposes, we will just focus on the ones that can be defined in a DTD.

- CDATA: Regular text
- Enumerated values: A list of values that you must use; no other values are acceptable.
- ID: A unique identifier
- IDREF: A pointer to an ID, helpful when making a link to the element that has that ID
- IDREFS: Multiple references to different ID's
- NMTOKEN: A name token—essentially a value that starts with a number

- NMTOKENS: Several name tokens

- ENTITY: The name of a predefined entity, usually a pointer to a file or character that lives outside of the XML document, and must be brought back in by the parser or browser

- ENTITIES: Several entities

- NOTATION: A file format, such as jpg or gif.

If the attribute value is of the type CDATA …

You can use any character defined in your encoding system; the default is the Unicode system known as UTF-8.

But you must not use the ampersand, less-than character, greater-than character, apostrophe, or double quote. For these, you should use the predefined entities.

For the ampersand character itself (&)	&amp;
For the less-than character (<)	&lt;
For the greater-than character (>)	&gt;
For the apostrophe (')	&apos;
For the double-quotes character (")	&quot;

You may also use entities that refer the parser to **characters** in an International Standards Organization list (for characters not in your encoding system). (More later).

Caution: You may not use entities that refer to external files.

Examples of valid attribute values for the attributes honorific and suffix, when the value type is CDATA.

These are start tags for PersonName elements.

```
<PersonName honorific="Mr."
suffix="Jr.">
<PersonName honorific="Señor"
suffix="Magnifico">
<PersonName honorific="The Right
Honorable" suffix="III">
```

Challenge on elements and attributes

Write the complete start tag, content, and end tag for a series of Product elements. The Product element has an attribute Internal.Description, with values of the type CDATA. Here are the products and their internal descriptions:

Product	Internal Description
Orsay	CD imported from Montparnasse > Multi media, Paris, France
Bauhaus	CD imported from Moholy & Nagy Productions, Berlin, Germany
Virtual Visit	CD out of stock
Sunflowers	Print "remainder"
Impressions	Print available at 'deep discount'

Answer:

```
<Product Internal.Description="CD
imported from Montparnasse &gt;
Multimedia, Paris,
France">Orsay</Product>
<Product Internal.Description="CD
imported from Moholy &amp; Nagy
Productions, Berlin,
Germany">Bauhaus</Product>
<Product Internal.Description="CD out
of stock">Virtual Visit</Product>
<Product Internal.Description="Print
&quot;remainder&quot;">Sunflowers</Pro
duct>
<Product Internal.Description="Print
available at &apos;deep
discount&apos;">Impressions</Product>
```

When an attribute value is of the type enumerated value ...

- Pick one of the values in the predefined list. Enumerated, here, just means listed. You must use one of the OK values, and nothing else.

- Make sure that your text matches the value in the list exactly, letter by letter.

- Match the case exactly.

These values must be legal XML **name tokens**. That is, the values may start with any character that would be valid in an attribute name, and then they should contain only valid name characters: any Unicode letter, number, underscore, hyphen, period, or colon.

Examples of valid values for the attribute of honorific when predefined to have only the following values: Mr | Ms | Dr | Rev

```
<PersonName honorific="Mr">
<PersonName honorific="Ms">
```

Examples of invalid values for the attribute of honorific when predefined to have only those values.

```
<PersonName honorific="Mr.">
<PersonName honorific="Herr Doktor">
```

Examples of valid enumeration attributes for the attribute marital.status:

```
<employee marital.status="married">
<employee marital.status="divorced">
<employee marital.status="single">
```

Challenge on enumerated values:

Write PersonName start tags for three people using the attribute Priority, with predefined values of VIP, Low.Value, and Risk.

Answer

```
<PersonName Priority="VIP">
<PersonName Priority="Low.Value">
<PersonName Priority="Risk">
```

When an attribute value is of the type ID ...

The value must be a unique identifier for this particular element. The ID must be a valid XML name; that is, the first character must be an underscore or letter; following characters may be letters, numbers, underscores, hyphens, periods or (in some cases) a colon. An illegal value would be a Social Security Number, because it begins with a number.

The value must be unique within the document:

- Every time you create a new element of this type, within this document, you must have a new ID value.

- An ID attribute can have only one value—to ensure uniqueness.

- Generally, if an element has an ID attribute, you must include the value. (Generally).

Examples of valid values for the attribute Primary.Key for the element Class.

```
<Class Primary.Key="English101a">
<Class Primary.Key="French54z">
<Class Primary.Key="Chemistry450a">
```

Examples of invalid values for the attribute Primary.Key for the element Class.

```
<Class Primary.Key="101Englisha">
<Class Primary.Key="—French54z">
<Class Primary.Key="….Chem450a">
```

Challenge on the data type ID:

Which of the following values would be invalid for an attribute of the type ID?

10106

Framis100

$450.56

Answer

Invalid values: 10106, $450.56

When the attribute value is of the type IDREF or IDREFS...

The value must match the value of an ID attribute somewhere else within the same document. The IDREF attribute refers to an ID; that is, it points to an element that has that unique identifier. For example, you might have a unique ID for a course, and then point to that course in the record for a student in that course, using an IDREF. In this way, you could have software locate all the students who are enrolled in that course.

Example of a valid value for the attribute ClassID for the element Course.

```
<Course ClassID="English101a">
```

Example of a valid value for the attribute ClassIDREF for the element Student.

```
<Student ClassIDREF="English101a">
```

Therefore the value in an IDREF must follow the rules for an ID value. Those are the rules for a valid XML name (starting with an underscore or letter, followed by letters, numbers, underscores, hyphens, periods, or a colon).

For several values (IDREFs) just put white space between them.

Examples of valid values for the attribute ClassIDREFS for the element Student.

```
<Student ClassIDREFS="English101a
French54z Chemistry450a">
```

Challenge on IDs and IDREFS

Within the element Patient, there is an element Prescription, which has an attribute PayerIDREFS, of the type IDREFS. Write the start tags for a Patient and the Prescription, which is being paid by two companies, whose IDs are HMO115 and HMO223.

Answer:

```
<Patient>
<Prescription PayerIDREFS="HMO115
HMO223">
```

When the attribute value is of the type **NMTOKEN** or **NMTOKENS** ...

You use an NMTOKEN when a regular XML name won't do, because the values you want to include must begin with something other than a letter or underscore.

The NMTOKEN value must contain only letters, numbers, underscores, hyphens, periods or colons. (The valid characters for an XML name).

You can start the NMTOKEN value with any of those characters (because Name Tokens free up the first character, whereas regular XML names can only start with an underscore or letter).

Unlike a value of the CDATA type, a NMTOKEN value cannot include white space, or other punctuation.

Examples of valid values for the attribute ISBN (with data type **NMTOKEN**) for the element Book.

```
<Book ISBN="978-1684220588">
<Book ISBN="978-0940450271">
```

If the type is NMTOKENS, put white space between the NMTOKENS.

Examples of valid values for the attribute Model (with data type **NMTOKENS**) for the element Movingbox.

```
<Movingbox Type="Mirrorbox"
Model="4565-S 4768-M 5890-L">
```

Challenge on **NMTOKENS**

Which of the following would be valid values for an attribute of the type NMTOKEN?

&More

%ofProfit

897

History

*Major

Ease of Use

"Discount"

Answer: Valid values: 897 and History

When an attribute value is of the type ENTITY or ENTITIES ...

1. Begin with ampersand (&).

2. Put the entity name, defined in the DTD (a valid XML name).

3. End with a semicolon (;).

If the attribute is defined as an ENTITY, then you must use this ugly set of markup, which is defined in the DTD. For example, &warning; is an entity called **warning**, and, in the DTD, points to a specific chunk of text or a symbol that the parser will drop in any time you happen to say &warning; in your XML document.

Examples of values of the type ENTITY:

&percent;   percent sign

¥   yen symbol

©   copyright symbol

&terms;   boilerplate Terms and Conditions

If the attribute is defined as ENTITIES, you can have several entities separated by white space.

Example of values for the attribute Inequality in the element Measure, using the entity references.
```
<Measure Inequality="&lt; &gt;">
```

When an attribute value is of the type NOTATION ...

You are referring to non-XML data, such as the file format for an image (which cannot be parsed) or an application (which would confuse the heck out of the parser, too). The notation information identifies the file format for the benefit of the browser that must display or run the file.

You get the actual notation from the DTD, where each of these file types must be defined. Usually, these are common suffixes such as jpg, bmp, doc, or gif.

Examples of values for the attribute Filetype in the element Image, using the notations defined in the DTD.
```
<Image Filetype="jpg">
<Image Filetype="bmp">
```

Summary of the data types for attribute values

For this data type	You write this kind of value.
CDATA	Regular text. (Character data, including any characters in the encoding you use, such as numbers, letters, punctuation, white spaces.)
Enumerated	One of the values explicitly defined in the DTD, such as Fulltime, Parttime, Retired. You cannot use any other value. (Sometimes known as an enumerated list).
ID	A unique identifier, such as a serial number, or primary key. This text string must conform to the rules for an element name. The first character must be a letter or underscore or a colon (in exceptional circumstances). Used to identify an element to which you expect to link.
IDREF	The value in the ID attribute of another element to which you want to refer, as when making a link. You are pointing to the element that the user will visit, when he or she clicks the link.
IDREFS	Several IDs, separated by space characters.
NMTOKEN	A name token—a text string that follows XML rules for names of elements, except that the first character can be any character that you could use elsewhere in a valid name (numbers, underscore, hyphen, period, and, in some circumstances, the colon). Most useful for values that start with a number.
NMTOKENS	Several name tokens, separated by space characters.
ENTITY	The name of a pre-defined entity, usually, a reference to a character, piece of boilerplate, or external file. Entities take the form: ampersand, name, semicolon. For example: '
ENTITIES	Several entities, separated by space characters.
NOTATION	A file format defined somewhere in the DTD, such as jpg, bmp, or gif.

The DTD or schema defines the kind of data that can go into an attribute's value.

Review on data types

For each item create four things:

1. Invent a name for the element.

2. Invent a name for the attribute.

3. Identify the type of value you would expect to use for the attribute value.

4. Create the start tag for the element, putting in a valid attribute with that type of value.

Items:

- A person's Social Security Number.

- An expression that has only three values: equal sign, greater than, and less than.

- The filetype of an image.

- A slew of keywords describing a product.

- The internal cost of goods for a product (without a dollar sign).

- A list of predefined references to external files.

- A serial number.

- An invoice number

- A pointer to another element within the document, indicating where the link will take you.

7e. Check to make sure you have included any required or fixed attributes.

Attributes may be required, optional, or fixed. Defined in the DTD, these parameters are called attribute defaults, because they tell a validating parser what to do if the attribute does not appear in the start tag.

- If an attribute is REQUIRED, it must appear with every instance of the element. And, of course, it must have a valid value.

- If an attribute is IMPLIED, it may or may not appear. It is optional.

- If an attribute is FIXED, it may or may not appear, but if it does appear, its value must be the specific value assigned in the DTD.

When values come and go:

- A REQUIRED attribute must appear every time its element appears. The value may change from one element to another, or there may be a default value. The default value is not automatically inserted. Even if there is a default value assigned, you may have to enter this value yourself, or another one.

- IMPLIED and FIXED attributes are both optional.

- If an IMPLIED attribute does not appear in the document, but the DTD assigns it a default value, then the parser may insert the attribute along with the default value before passing the parsed document along to the browser. Because this is all a matter for software, you usually do not have to worry about the default value. But knowing what it is may tip you off to times when you ought to include an IMPLIED attribute, because you may need something other than the default value.

- A FIXED attribute has only one value, ever, because it is, well, fixed.

Challenge on attribute defaults

For the element Employee, guess which of the following attributes would be REQUIRED, IMPLIED, or FIXED:

Social.Security.Number

Number.of.Children

Include.in.Payroll

Second.Home

Backup.Phone

Answers

(Your answers may vary, depending on what you assume about the situation).

REQUIRED: Social.Security.Number

IMPLIED: Number.of.Children, Second.Home, Backup.Phone

FIXED: Include.in.Payroll

Review of attributes

1. What is the role of an attribute?

2. What are valid first characters for an attribute name?

3. For the rest of the name?

4. What are the delimiters around the attribute value?

5. What goes into a value of the type CDATA?

6. Give examples of two things you may not put into a CDATA value.

7. What are enumerated values, and why do you imagine a designer would decide to use them?

8. What is the relationship between an element with an ID attribute and an element with an IDREF attribute, with the value of the first element's ID?

9. When would a designer choose to use values of the type NMTOKEN?

10. If a value must be an entity, what delimits the entity name?

11. What values might appear in a NOTATION?

12. What is the difference between a REQUIRED and an IMPLIED attribute?

8. An entity reference lets you include reserved or unusual characters or bring in an external file, within element content or attribute values.

Entity Reference

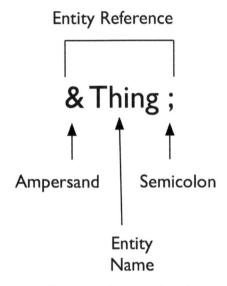

Ampersand   Semicolon

Entity
Name

An entity is a **thingamajig**—something or other that exists outside of the XML document.

In some cases, the entity is a **character**, living in a list somewhere on the site of a standards organization.

In the special case of XML **reserved characters**, the entities live in the parser, which recognizes the entity references, and, before sending the file along to the browser, puts the correct characters into the text.

Other entities include **external files** such as images, sounds, and video clips.

All the entities that you can use in your XML document are defined in the DTD (except for the ones standing for the reserved characters, which you don't have to define in the DTD, because the parser knows them by heart).

In your document, you point to one of those entities by using a strange chunk of markup called an **entity reference**.

8a) Start the entity reference with an ampersand.

8b) Insert a valid XML name.

The name of the entity has been defined in your DTD.

8c) End with a semicolon.

The XML creators figured that no one would ever write a word that begins with an ampersand and ends with a semicolon, so they chose this odd sequence to represent entity references. Later, when parsed, the entity reference is replaced with the actual character or image at the other end, when the document is passed along to the browser or another application, for further processing.

For an XML reserved character, use a predefined entity reference

XML uses some characters to indicate the beginning or end of a segment within its markup. These characters are "reserved" for XML. So when we want to use one of these characters in our content, we must reach for a workaround that the XML team has created for us—a "predefined" entity reference.

In a well-formatted document, use one of these predefined XML entity references as a substitute for a reserved character:

For the ampersand character itself (&)	&amp;
For the less-than character (<)	&lt;
For the greater-than character (>)	&gt;
For the apostrophe (')	&apos;
For the double-quotes character (")	&quot;

Examples of entity references for reserved characters:

```
AT&amp;T
Possessive="Jack&apos;s"
<Result>The result of the calculation
is AB&gt;CD. </Result>
```

Etymological curiosity: In the old days, one way of typing a reserved character was to hold down the Escape key and then type the character's key—resulting in a different character, as far as the computer was concerned. This process came to be known as "escaping" the character. And you may hear people talking about these entity references as "escape characters."

For an entity that is an external file, such as an image, use the same syntax (ampersand, name, semicolon).

The entity is defined in the DTD. For instance, a picture might be defined as &snow; and in the DTD we'd see the path to that file. The browser would look up the path to that file, fetch the file, and insert the image into the document.

> **Example:** An entity reference to an external file showing a picture of snow:
>
> ```
> <destination type="weekend"
> season="winter">
> &snow;
> </destination>
> ```

Challenge on entity references

For an attribute's value, write the following using entity references to avoid the prohibited characters:

B&B

9>7

Bar&Grill

<tag>

100>83

R&B

"kitschy"

Lands'End

Answers

B&B

9>7

Bar&Grill

<tag>

100>83

R&B

"kitschy"

Lands'End

For a character that you can't type, or that your XML editor would not otherwise recognize, identity the number system and the code for that character within an entity reference.

1. Look the character up in the ISO/IEC 10646 character set.

2. Find the decimal or hexadecimal number for the character.

3. Start the entity reference with an ampersand.

4. Enter a pound sign (for the decimal number) or a pound sign followed by an x (for the hexadecimal number).

5. Enter the decimal or hexadecimal number.

6. End with a semicolon.

You can use these entity references—sometimes known as character references— in element content and attribute values.

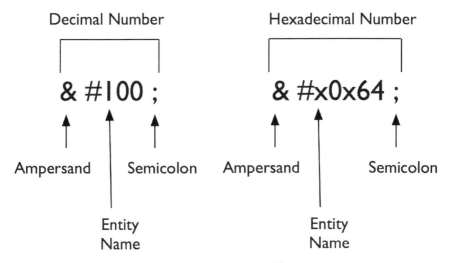

Decimal Number   Hexadecimal Number

& #100 ;   & #x0x64 ;

Ampersand   Semicolon   Ampersand   Semicolon

Entity Name   Entity Name

Examples of Besançon and Überammergau using decimal references to the c cedilla and the umlaut U.

```
<city>Besan&#231;on</city>
<city>&#220;berammergau</city>
```

Review of entity references

1. What is the difference between an entity, and an entity reference?

2. If you were going to write an entity reference in your XML document, what characters would start and end the reference?

3. When writing ordinary text in an XML document, why do you need to use an entity reference instead of an actual less-than character?

4. Do "predefined" entities need to be defined in the DTD?

5. If the DTD describes an entity as a file path pointing to an external file, such as an image, what is the syntax for the entity reference?

6. In what circumstances would you have to look up a character in the ISO/IEC 10646 character set?

7. In that character set, what are the two number systems used?

8. If you are writing an entity reference pointing to a character in the ISO/IEC 10646 character set, what components of the syntax resemble the markup for other entity references?

9. What is the secret code for hexadecimal numbers, in this situation?

10. What are four examples of entities?

9. CDATA sections contain text you don't want the parser to read.

A CDATA section contains unparsed character data. Huh? The markup tells the parser, "Just skip to the end of this section, without reading or parsing any of the contents, please." Why would this be useful? CDATA sections let you pass along text that contains a lot of restricted characters without translating those into entity references—any text that you want to preserve untouched.

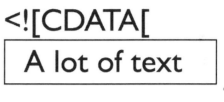

Like a comment, a CDATA section gets passed over by the parser. Unlike a comment, a CDATA section offers real content to the user. The parser just passes along anything within the CDATA section, unexamined, and unchanged, to the next application (usually the browser).

9a) Start the section with <!

Alert! Exciting section coming up! This could be as important as one of those comments, which also begin with these two characters.

9b) Put in an opening square bracket and insert the keyword CDATA (all caps) and another opening square bracket.

You are putting a nice set of delimiters around the raw content, isolating it from the well-organized, correctly marked-up content before and after the CDATA section.

The first square bracket distinguishes this markup from the comment (which puts two hyphens right after the exclamation point).

CDATA is a keyword, recognized by the parser.

The second opening square bracket heralds the content itself.

9c) Type any text you want, including prohibited characters.

Remember: the main reason to use a CDATA section is to get these reserved characters past the parser. (Or maybe you just want to keep the text exactly as it stands, without any other interference by the parser).

9d) Put]]> to close out the CDATA section.

Now the parser wakes up, and starts parsing again.

Example of legal CDATA section:

```
<![CDATA[
So you conclude that CB>DE, and FD<DE,
or, to quote Euclid, "CB is proved to
be larger than DE, & FD is less than
DE. QED." Please check your work.
]]>
```

When to use CDATA sections, and when not to

CDATA sections are a form of cheating. They get around the parser, but in doing so, they give up one of the major advantages of XML. The pieces of content inside the CDATA section cannot be identified by the parser as discrete components, because nothing inside the section is considered markup. Even if you happen to put a tag in there, the parser will never see it.

Therefore, if you are displaying large chunks of HTML or XML code, you may want to use CDATA sections, so that you don't have to keep inserting entity references every time you hit a less-than character.

Caution: Don't get carried away. There is one sequence of characters you must not put inside a CDATA section—the ones that signal the end of the CDATA section. Just don't include two closing square brackets followed by a greater-than character, and your content will be OK.

Review of CDATA sections

1. What kind of markup is the word CDATA?

2. What parts of the CDATA markup resemble the markup for a comment?

3. What markup surrounds the actual content?

4. What are some circumstances in which you would need to use a CDATA section?

5. What is the major disadvantage to using CDATA sections?

10. Comments let you pass along reminders to yourself or team members—without users listening in.

You can place comments in the prolog, right after the document element, or inside any element's content. The parser ignores anything in the comment. The user never sees what you say in the comment.

<!--Comment-->

10a. Start with a less-than character, exclamation point, and two hyphens.

Make sure you have turned off the auto-correction that transforms double hyphens into dashes.

10b. Put in your text.

Remember: Do not try to put a double hyphen inside the comment!

10c. End with two hyphens, and a greater-than character.

Use comments for notes to yourself, your user, or some other human being.

Once you are inside a comment, you can write any darn thing you want.

The XML parser ignores the comments, and does not bother to pass them along to the browser (ensuring your partial privacy). The parser does not expand entity references within a comment, or act on any tags you may have inserted.

Where to put comments

You can put comments anywhere you want inside an XML document except in a CDATA section, because, there, the parser treats the whole comment as just another part of the text. In effect, you have to have the parser turned on to register a comment as a comment.

Examples of comments:

```
<!--File Name: catalog.xml -->
<!--Remember to review for accuracy.-->
<!—Archive_Date: July 4, 2025 -->
```

11. A processing Instruction (PI) passes an instruction or command to an application.

Processing Instruction

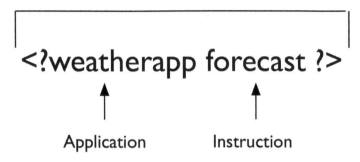

The PI markup warns the parser not to tinker with the material inside the PI, because the browser will need to know the name of the application to call, and the exact instructions to pass to that application.

You can place PIs anywhere you can place a comment—in the prolog, in the body, between elements, or inside any element's content.

11a. Start the Processing Instruction with a less-than character and a question mark.

11b. Identify the application or applet you want to take action.

11c. Put in the instructions that will make sense to that application.

The exact nature of the instructions varies from application to application.

Some instructions have name-value pairs that look like attribute names and their values. Other applications demand a long string of parameters.

11d. End with a question mark and a greater-than character.

A Processing Instruction ends with a question mark and angle bracket. It does **not** have a following end tag, perhaps because its content lives within the instructions, and once you finish writing the instructions, that's it.

Caution: You must not place a PI **within** a tag.

142

Examples of Processing Instructions:

```
<?Jpscript01 emphasize="yes"?>
<?robots index="yes" follow="no"?>
<?xsl-stylesheet type="text/css"
href="slick.css"?>
```

Challenge on the components of the body of an XML document

Label every component you recognize:

<book>

<book code="P100">

</book>

<locator keyword="big"/>

<?xml version="1.0"?>

<!--This section needs work.-->

<![CDATA[Therefore, he says, "A>B."]]>

&#174;

&#xAF4;

<catalog>

<DVD source="France" vendor="Oiseau">

</DVD>

<locator trigger="primary"/>

<?xml version="1.0"?>

<!--Here we draw data down.-->

<?calendarapp SELECT date FROM sked.cal?>

&#124;

&#xAF4;

Answers

Element start tag, element with code attribute and its value, element end tag, empty element, empty element with attribute for keyword and value, xml declaration, comment, CDATA section, decimal character reference, hex character reference

Element start tag, element start tag with two attributes and their values, element end tag, empty element tag, empty element with attribute and value, xml declaration, comment, processing instruction, decimal character reference, hex character reference

Epilog

An epilog lets you add Comments or Processing Instructions. (Not content).

The epilog begins after you close the root element. Generally, parsers stop paying attention at this point, so your epilog may be totally ignored.

That's why epilogs are not recommended.

Tim Bray, one of the authors of XML 1.0, considers the epilog "a real design error."

Better solution: Put Comments earlier, and place Processing Instructions near the data they relate to.

FAQ

In general

Q: Are you as persnickety as XML seems to be? Do you always get this stuff right the first time?

> A: No, I make plenty of mistakes. In fact, that's why I had to come up with this step-by-step method for learning all the little twists and turns of XML markup. Some people have a gift for code; I don't. I have to walk through the markup one baby step at a time, and even then the parser barks at me.

Elements

Q: Why is the top element in the hierarchy called the root element when a tree's roots are at the bottom, underground?

> A: You're right about the tree. But in the XML world, a tree structure grows downward from a root in the sky, branching out as it goes down toward the ground.
>
> Less important elements appear lower down. But at the top is the, uh, well, the root.
>
> Perhaps it would help to think of the root element as fundamental, basic, the ur element, the beginning and ending of all other elements in the document. You can see why some folks just call this the document element, because it contains all the other elements in the document.

Q: Do we have to indent these sub-elements for the parser?

> A: No, the indents are to help us humans read the text. The parser ignores this kind of white space.

Q: Couldn't I just have an XML document with elements, and nothing else?

> A: Sure. Elements are the heart of the document because they carry the meaning. But other components, such as entities, contribute little pieces of content; attributes help software manipulate the content; and processing instructions invoke more software, to insert live content, or massage the existing content.

Q: Do I just make these element names up as I go along?

> A: No, the team that created the DTD spelled out each element's name. Your job, then, is to use that name exactly as defined— so that the parser will recognize your tags when it looks them up in the DTD.

Q: What if I leave off that closing angle bracket? I don't always get my tags just right in HTML, and the browsers seem to handle the mess OK.

> A: In XML, if you leave out even one little tiny piece of punctuation, the parser pronounces your document ill-formed, and refuses to display anything, or just shows raw text. Because the parser insists that you follow the rules, its code can be much smaller than the code used to handle all the exceptions (read, mistakes) in HTML tagging. Hence, the XML parser is so lightweight it can live on a mobile device. Unfortunately, to take advantage of XML, you have to be very picky with your punctuation.

Q: So do I get the title "content provider" if I write in XML?

> A: Yes. A number of writers' lists debate whether you should call yourself a content provider when applying for jobs. Sure. Of course, someone has to actually write this stuff, to begin with. To write well, you need to enter an alpha state, groping toward meaning. But putting in tags requires a different state, one more akin to editing, a critical perspective, outside of the actual meaning, analyzing more than creating. You can think of markup as a second pass through the material. Or, in an XML editor, you can work in a WHAT YOU SEE IS WHAT YOU GET mode, then switch to view the tags…if necessary. In either view, you are creating content.

Q: If parsed character data is ordinary text, can I use the punctuation that XML uses?

> A: No. Don't put an ampersand (&) , two closing square brackets (]]), or a less-than character (<) into the parsed character data. (These are markup delimiters). Instead use entity references (markup that points to the characters you want inserted).

Q: Do I really need an end tag? In HTML I leave those out, sometimes, and I can't see that it makes much difference.

A: Yes, in XML you must include the end tags, to show the parser exactly where the element stops. Otherwise, the parser will just balk, and stop processing your document. (HTML parsers are much more forgiving). Learning to include the end tags is one of the hardest aspects of XML for hardcore HTML coders.

Q: If an empty tag has an attribute pointing to some image, why do they call the tag empty?

A: Because, from the parser's point of view, there is no text to analyze. The pointer gets passed along to the browser, to bring in that image, but from XML's parochial point of view, there is no content. Remember that the empty tag is really a shorthand expression, standing for a start tag and an end tag (with nothing in-between).

Q: So the root element is a parent?

A: Yes, most of the time, because in most XML documents, the root element has subordinate components, which are considered its children. In those documents, then, the root element is a parent. In rare cases you may have a root element with no children, but that kind of document is extremely simple-minded, and not very useful.

Q: What exactly is proper nesting? This sounds like a Puritan talking about getting married, and buying a house, before settling down.

A: Proper nesting means following the structure laid out in the DTD. That content model shows what elements are components of another element, and which elements should appear in a sequence. Two rules, then: (1) You must close a child element before you close its parent. (2) If one element follows another, you must close the first before starting the next.

Attributes

Q: What would I use an attribute for?

A: Attributes let the team keep information about an object right inside the object itself: data like the author's name, date of modification, file location, or owner. In addition, attributes allow you to provide information to be used by software such as search engines: subject keywords, natural language, product numbers.

148

Q: What the heck is a data type?

> A: It's a kind of data. Big help, huh? Well, the term comes from data modeling, a discipline used by people creating databases and large systems. When programmers are developing databases, for example, they need to know whether a field contains a date, a number, or a chunk of text. Why? Because if you have to sort records according to the values in that field, you run a different algorithm against the values, depending on the type of data there. You sort dates one way, numbers another way, and raw text in a third way. Because they are anticipating how software will be using that value, the DTD team defines the data type for an attribute's value. Usually, the data type makes sense, and you do not have a lot of difficulty following the guidelines. Just be aware that each attribute's value has a data type.

Q: How come some of the data types have names in all capital letters, but the enumerated list does not?

> A: XML puts its own keywords in ALL CAPS. With the enumerated list as a type, the XML designers decided that it was more important to provide the list of acceptable values than to label the data type. In the DTD, then, the data type is implied when the definition of the attribute shows a list of text items separated by pipe characters (meaning *or*), as values. If you look at all the other kinds of values, you will see that they all describe a type, but none of them actually specifies the values. The enumerated type does that, offering a list.

Attribute Values

Q: What if I have a bunch of IDs that begin with numbers?

> A: You must convert them so they begin with a letter or underscore, if you want to pass inspection. A nuisance, and an indication of the crude nature of the validation performed by an XML parser these days.

Q: Do NMTOKENS have something to do with New Mexico?

> A: No, this is a keyword meaning Name Tokens.

Q: Isn't a name a token, I mean, a stand-in, for the real thing?

> A: Yes, but the team creating XML set very strict rules about legal XML names (they must begin with a letter or

underscore). To allow values that had a different first character, the XML team invented, uh, well, not names exactly, but kind of like names, you know, token names, or, well, Name Tokens.

Q: What is a FIXED value? Does that mean it was broken, and now it has been repaired?

A: No, FIXED means that the value is established for all eternity. You must use the same value for this attribute every time the attribute appears (but the attribute itself may or may not appear). The DTD spells out what that value is.

Q: What is the difference between an ID and an IDREF?

A: The first identifies an element—a particular chunk of text, say—and the other refers to, or points to, that element. The ID is the target, and the IDREF is the link. If I click the IDREF, on a Web page, I will go to the element with the ID referred to.

Entity References

Q: What's an entity?

A: An entity is one of several things: a chunk of text defined in the DTD, or a special character, or an external file containing something like an image, a sound, or a video clip.

Q: If an entity can be a character, a piece of text, or a whole file, why did the XML designers lump all those things together, calling them all entities?

A: Hey, think of the XML designers' situation. They started with the premise that an XML document should be raw text, so it could be read by almost any software anywhere. Then they said, well, but a few of those characters must be reserved for our own use, so if a writer wants to include one of those, the writer will have to, uh, point to the character, rather than just typing it in. And if you want to use some boilerplate text over and over, you will need some kind of way of pointing to that. And, eventually, the page may need to have some pictures, so you'll need a way to point to those. Notice what all these situations have in common: pointing outside the XML document to something or other. What should we call that thingee? Well, thing does not sound very elegant. So let's use a fancier word for thing, like, say, *entity*.

Q: If I just use a picture in one XML document, would I have to make up an entity in the standard DTD for every picture I might ever use?

> A: No. Remember the internal subset of the DTD? You could start off the DOCTYPE declaration pointing to the external DTD, then go on to define one more entity, for this particular picture, in the internal subset.

Q: How do I do that?

> A: Creating entities in the DTD is another story. For now, all you need to know is the form of the entity reference. In another book, we'll get into DTD-making, which is more fun than getting a root canal.

Q: So where do I find this ISO/IEC 10646 character set?

> A: The International Standards Organization offers downloadable copies of many of their standards, including this one. (Caution: These are large, slow files). See:

>> http://standards.iso.org/ittf/PubliclyAvailableStandards/index.ht ml

Q: What does that set look like?

> A: It's sorted in different ways. For instance, sorted alphabetically by name, part of it looks like this:

2708 AIRPLANE

2135 ALEF SYMBOL

232E ALL AROUNDPROFILE

224C ALL EQUAL TO

2387 ALTERNATIVE KEY SYMBOL

0026 AMPERSAND

CDATA Sections

Q: Once I get into a CDATA section, it sounds like I can relax. Is that right?

> A: Yes, the parser is no longer looking over your shoulder, as you go through the CDATA section, so you can write any darn thing you want—until the end.

Comments

Q: Do you have any comments to make on comments?

A: Yes—include more of them. The more comments you put into the document as you create it, the faster you will be able to figure out what the heck you were doing, when you come back to the document in six months. Plus, your comments may help the next writer, or some programmer in the future, to figure out what you were thinking.

Processing Instructions

Q: I see that the XML declaration starts with the same <? as the PI. Is the XML declaration a PI?

A: Technically, no. But you might think of the XML declaration as a very special case of processing instruction, because it can only appear at the start of the prolog (whereas a regular PI can appear anywhere in the document). Also, parsers pass along all processing instructions to the applications, but the XML declaration gives information to the parser itself, so there is no need for it to pass the declaration along. (Of course, a few parsers get confused, and send the XML declaration right along to the browser).

Epilog

Q: Is there any way you indicate that the epilog is beginning?

A: Yes, you put in the end tag for your root element. Anything after that is, well, just an epilog.

Q: What's next?

A: Now that you have learned the tags for an XML document, the next challenge is reading and writing the DTD or schema that defines all those tags. But that's the subject for another book.

Glossary

Attribute	Description of an element. Consists of a name, such as *price*, and a particular value, such as *retail*. Appears in the start tag for the element it characterizes. Example: <product price="retail">
Body	Required part of an XML document, because it contains the root element. May contain other elements, with their attributes, plus comments, entity references, processing instructions, and CDATA sections.
CDATA	Keyword for an attribute type and section with almost any characters permitted. Example: <![CDATA[text]]>
Character code	Numbers assigned to a set of characters. Example: Unicode.
Character encoding	The way the numbers are represented, in character codes; part of an XML declaration. Example: <XML version='1.0' encoding='UTF-16' standalone='no'>
Character entities	Characters you cannot type, referred to by entity references. Example: ç
Child element	An element that fits into a larger element as a component; it belongs to the higher-level element, as a child to a parent. Example: <book> <title>Biggie</title> </book>
Comment	Expression of your opinions, reminders, notes to yourself, without the parser reading them. Example: <!--comment-->
Content	Data that communicates meaningful information to the user. Example:

	<name>Jonathan Price</name>
Data type	Criterion for an attribute value, specifying characters allowed. Examples: CDATA, ENTITY, ID, IDREF, NMTOKEN, NOTATION.
DOCTYPE	Announces what type of document this is, and points to the DTD. Example: <!DOCTYPE MESSAGE SYSTEM "http://www.example.com/message.dtd">
Document Type Definition (DTD)	Spells out the structure of an XML document of this type, defines tags for all elements, attributes, entities. May be included in document, or separate file. Example: <!DOCTYPE MESSAGE [<!ELEMENT MESSAGE ANY>]>
Element	Item that contains content that will be visible to the reader, placed between a start tag and an end tag. The tags carry the name of the element—the class or category of information contained in the element, such as "product." A particular element is an instance of that class. The start tag may also contain attributes, describing this particular element. Example: <product type="whistle"> Whizzer </product>
Empty element	An element that contains no text content, but may carry an attribute pointing to an external file such as an image. Example: <image file="http://www.aol.com/rhino.jpg"/>
Encoding	A way to represent a set of characters; a part of the XML declaration. Example: <XML version='1.0' encoding='UTF-16' standalone='no'>
Entity references	Pointers to things that cannot appear in regular text, such as images; characters on standard lists; and external files. Example: &#231; &snow;

Enumerated values	Attribute values from a list in the DTD. Example: <zoo type="adventure">
Epilog	Unnecessary and disregarded part of an XML document; may hold comments and processing instructions; appears after the body.
Escape characters	Entity references standing for characters that are reserved by XML for its own use, such as the less-than symbol; replaced with the actual characters during parsing. Example: <
External DTD	A Document Type Definition that exists in a separate file, pointed to by the XML declaration in the document. <!DOCTYPE MESSAGE SYSTEM "http://www.example.com/ message.dtd">
FIXED	An attribute whose value is fixed, once and for all, in the DTD, and never changes. Example: <printer inventory="yes">
Formal Public Identifier (FPI)	The description of a DTD that is commonly known. Example: <DOCTYPE book PUBLIC "-//OASIS//DTD DocBook V.3.1//EN">
Generic identifier (GI)	The name of something, such as an element. Example: <name>
ID	Attribute type requiring a unique value for each instance of the element in a document; an identifier. Example: <employee badge='A14'>
IDREF	Attribute type requiring, as a value, an ID within the same document. Example: <see.also link='A14'>
IMPLIED	Attribute that is optional, not required. Example: <order gift.wrap='finest'>
ISO-8859-1	An international standard for encoding of characters. Example: <xml version='1.0'

	encoding='ISO-8859-1' standalone='no'>
Namespace Declaration	A statement announcing a prefix to stand before an element name, indicating the location or namespace of its DTD. Example: <hr:employee xmlns:hr="http://www.example.com/hum.resources"/>
Namespace Identifier (NID)	An organization, standard, or generic name for the owner, creator, or source of the particular resource, such as a DTD or schema. Used in the rare circumstances when you are using a Uniform Resource Name to give the System location of the DTD in a DOCTYPE declaration. Example: If xyz.org is the owner of the DTD describing documents of the type featurelist, you might write: <!DOCTYPE featurelist SYSTEM "urn:xyz.org:featurelist.dtd" >
Nesting	A hierarchy defined in the DTD. When an element starts within another element, it must end within that same element. When the DTD says that one element comes after another, you must end the first before starting the next. The parser applies these rules to the XML document, and if there are any violations, pronounces the document "not well formed." Operations cease at that point. If the document is judged "well-formed," the parser proceeds to check to see if it is also valid.
NMTOKEN	A type of attribute value that can have, as its first character, any character that you could normally put in a valid XML name, followed by other valid name characters. Example: <staff ssn="123456677">

NOTATION	A type of attribute value that indicates a file type. The notations are defined in the DTD. Example: <video.description type='mov'>
Parser	A utility that checks an incoming XML document in two passes. First it confirms that the tags follow XML rules and that they are well nested. If so, the document is pronounced "well formed," and the parser undertakes the second pass. It now compares the tags, their markup, and their organization with the DTD, to make sure that they all match. If so, the parser declares the document "valid," and passes it along to the browser to display, using the stylesheet pointed to in the document's prolog.
Path	In a DOCTYPE declaration, when giving the SYSTEM location, indicates the location of the DTD file. Example: <!DOCTYPE procedure SYSTEM "http://www.aol.com /procedure.dtd">
Processing Instruction	Gives a command to an application, for processing. Example: <?weatherapp SELECT forecast?>
Prolog	The first part of an XML document, required only if you are going to provide a DOCTYPE declaration, so a parser can check that the document is valid. Starts with an XML declaration.
	Example: <?xml version='1.0' encoding='UTF-16' standalone='no'?>
	<!DOCTYPE concept SYSTEM "http://www.example.com/concept.dtd">
Protocol	The method by which the parser or browser can access a file such as the DTD. Used in the DOCTYPE declaration in a SYSTEM location using a URL.

Examples: http, ftp.

<!DOCTYPE brochure SYSTEM "http://www.maj.com/brochure.dtd">

PUBLIC

One way of indicating the location of a DTD; assumes the location is generally known, and provides a Formal Public Identifier, such as the one for DocBook, followed by a more conventional system location. Example:

<DOCTYPE PUBLIC "-//OASIS//DTD DocBook V.3.1//EN" "http://www. oasis.org/docbook.dtd">

REQUIRED

Keyword for an attribute that must be included each time you create an instance of its element. Example: <employee badge='a123'>

Root element

The only required component in an XML document. Any other elements are nested within it. Example, where *book* is the root element.

<book>

    <title>Leaves of Grass

    </title>

    <author>Walt Whitman

    </author>

</book>

Standalone

An attribute in the XML declaration, indicating whether the document depends on an external DTD or not. Posed as an implied question. So, if the document depends on an outside DTD or schema, the answer is "No, this document is not standalone."

Example: <?xml version='1.0' encoding='UTF-8' standalone='no'?>

Start tag	First tag for an element. Includes the name of the class, such as *pricing*. May contain attributes describing the particular instance of that class, such as *retail* or *wholesale*. Example: <pricing type="retail" >
Stylesheet	A set of transformations and formats to apply to the material in the XML document; usually an external file, declared in the stylesheet instructions. Example: <?xml-stylesheet type="text/xsl" href="http://www.example.com/product.xsl"?>
SYSTEM	Specific location of the DTD, given in a DOCTYPE declaration. Example: <!DOCTYPE catalog SYSTEM "file:///user/local/xml/docbook/3.1/docbook.dtd">
Text class	A component in the Formal Public Identifier, saying what kind of a file the text is (usually a DTD or a stylesheet, either XSL or CSS), followed by a description of that file. Example: <DOCTYPE book PUBLIC "-//OASIS//DTD DocBook V.3.1//EN">
Unicode, UTF-8, UTF-16	A form of character encoding. XML parsers and UTF-16 assume UTF-8 character encoding if you do not specify something else in the XML declaration. UTF-8 and UTF-16 are two versions of Unicode; standard ASCII is a subset of UTF-8. Example: <?xml version='1.0' encoding='UTF-16' standalone='no'?>
Validation	Confirmation that the markup in the XML document matches what has been defined in the DTD or schema; that the sequence and hierarchy are as defined. If valid, the document is passed to the browser to display using the stylesheet named in the prolog.

Value	The description of an element, within the attribute. For example, the element "building" has an attribute "architect," with values such as Wright, Corbusier, Gehry. Within the start tag, the attribute name is followed by an equal sign, then single or double quotes, the particular value for this element, and closing single or double quotes. Example: <building architect= 'Wright'>
Version	In the XML declaration, this attribute identifies the edition of XML. Example: <?xml version='1.0' encoding='UTF-16' standalone='no'?>
Windows-1252	A form of character encoding spawned by many Microsoft applications. Example: <?xml version='1.0' encoding='windows-1252' standalone='no'?>
XML	A keyword reserved for XML's own use, so you cannot use it to begin an element name, attribute name, or value. But it is part of the XML declaration, and a stylesheet instruction. Example: <?xml version='1.0' encoding='EBCDIC' standalone='yes'?>
XML declaration	First line in a prolog, describing what version of XML you are using, saying what character encoding you are using, and telling the parser whether this document stands on its own, or depends on another file, such as an external DTD, for validation. Example: <?xml version='1.0' encoding='UTF-16' standalone='no'?>
XML name	A string of text that follows the rules for XML names (starting with an underscore or letter, followed by letters, numbers, underscores, periods, hyphens, and, occasionally, a colon). Example: <name>

XMLNS | An attribute indicating the namespace and prefix inside a Namespace Declaration. Example: <ship:head xmlns:ship= "http://www.usn.gov/shipping.terms"/>

XSLT | The eXtensible Stylesheet Language Transformation, a tool for creating stylesheets that both format and transform the content of the XML document.

Index

Punctuation

& (ampersand)
Entity reference for 123
ISO code 151
Predefined entity reference 135
Reserved character 31-32, 123, 135
Starting an attribute value of the type ENTITY 129
Starting an entity reference 115, 118, 134, 137
Unacceptable in some attribute values 120
Unacceptable in parsed character data 147

: (colon)
Acceptable (at times) within a value of the type ID 126
Acceptable in enumerated value 125
Acceptable in NMTOKEN or NMTOKENS 128
Separating the Namespace Identifier from the Namespace Specific String 78
Separating the namespace prefix from the element name 112
Separating the protocol from the path 77
Separating URN from the Namespace Identifier 78
Separating xmlns from prefix 79
Unacceptable in element name 112

= (equal sign)
Between attribute name and value 119, 120
In encoding attribute 66
In stylesheet instruction 86-87
In xmlns attribute 79
Unacceptable in element name 113

! (exclamation point)
In a CDATA tag 139, 153
In a comment tag 69, 141
In a DOCTYPE declaration 75
Unacceptable in element name 113

> (greater than sign or closing angle bracket)
Compared with usage in HTML 147
Delimiter 113
Ending a CDATA section 139
Ending a Comment 69, 141
Ending a DOCTYPE Declaration 83
Ending a Namespace Declaration 156
Ending an element tag 115-116, 147
Ending an empty element 117
Ending a Processing Instruction 70-71, 142
Ending a stylesheet processing instruction 86
Entity reference for 123
In XML Declaration 68
Predefined entity reference 135
Reserved character 31-32, 123, 135

Y

Z

Author's Note

Q: How did you get into writing about XML?

I regularly work in XML environments as a writer and consultant—gigantic web sites grinding away with content management software, mostly in ecommerce, high tech, and scientific research. I have been creating content for the Web for more than 20 years, mostly for large corporations, writing tips, FAQs, and task topics, helping to develop information architectures, refining customer assistance, and coaching teams on content strategy.

Q: What's your background?

I was a Latin major at Harvard, but when I discovered that I had run out of undergraduate courses, and might have to learn Greek, I backed out, and became an English major. I went to the Yale School of Drama as a playwright, and earned a Doctorate of Fine Arts, writing about Shakespeare's *King John* over in the English Department. I taught drama for two years at New York University, but quit to write full time.

In New York, I wrote articles for magazines like *Harper's, Reader's Digest*, and *TV Guide*. I co-authored a book on drama with John Lahr—*Life Show: How to See Theater in Life and Life in Theater*. And in other books (and a bunch of articles) I explored video art and TV commercials. At the same time, I was doing conceptual and video art in West Broadway Gallery, and concrete poetry wherever.

To make a little more money, I ran the Shakespeare Institute, a summer graduate program for teachers at the University of Bridgeport, and then taught at Rutgers. But when I heard that there was life west of the Hudson, I moved to California, where I discovered technical writing.

I spent four years as a Senior Technical Writer at Apple Computer, which was a little like being in graduate school: lots of intense, very bright people obsessing about obscure subjects (like laser printers, Chinese fonts, hypertext, and operating systems). I wrote a styleguide for the technical writers, called *How to Write an Apple Manual*, which morphed into *How to Write a Computer Manual*, which became, with the help of Henry Korman, Mick Renner, Linda Urban, and Adam Rochmes, *How to Communicate Technical Information*.

After graduating from Apple, I wrote a lot of help systems, and consulted with an A to Z of high-tech firms on electronic customer assistance, first within programs, then on the Web. I coach professional writing teams and give workshops on writing at conferences and at universities such as the University of California Extension at Santa Cruz. My wife Lisa and I have published *Hot Text: Web Writing that Works*, a book on how to write effectively for the Web.

For more info, see:

- Blog: http://museumzero.blogspot.com/

- Linked In: http://www.linkedin.com/in/JonathanReevePrice

- Amazon Author Page: https://www.amazon.com/author/jonathanprice

- Www.webwritingthatworks.com

Q: Where do you live, anyway?

My wife and I live in a small house overlooking the Rio Grande River, where it flows through New Mexico on its way to Texas and Mexico. We have two sons, Ben and Noah, who live near us. Our three Corgi dogs, Reggie, Sterling, and Jagger, run and bark to chase away hot air balloons.

Other books

Hot Text—Web Writing that Works! With Lisa Price. New Riders. 2002.

Special Edition Using FileMaker Pro 5, with Rich Coulombre, Que, 2000.

The Best of Online Shopping: The Prices' Guide to the Fastest and Easiest Stores on the Web. With Lisa Price. Ballantine. 1999.

Fun with Digital Imaging: The Official HP Guide. With Lisa Price. IDG. 1999.

Outlining Goes Electronic: A Study of the Impact of Media on our Understanding of the Role of Outlining in Virtual and Collaborative Conversations. ATTW Series, Ablex. 1999.

Windows 95 for Kids and Parents. With Lisa Price. IDG Books. 1998.

Discover Microsoft Home Essentials. With Lisa Price. IDG Books. 1997.

Trail Guide to America Online. Addison-Wesley. 1994.

The Virtual Playhouse for the Macintosh. Edited and written with a CD. Hayden Books. 1994.

ClarisWorks 2.0 for the Macintosh. with Brown, Outler, and Renner, South-Western Publishing. 1994.

How to Communicate Technical Information, with Henry Korman. Benjamin/Cummings. 1993.

FileMaker Pro for Windows, with Rich Coulombre. Addison-Wesley. 1993.

FileMaker Pro for the Macintosh, with Rich Coulombre. Addison-Wesley. 1992.

Using ClarisWorks, with Henry Korman, Adam Rochmes, and Linda Urban. South-Western Publishing. 1993.

Microsoft Works Tutorial and Applications. South-Western Publishing. 1990.

The MacWrite II Handbook and Toolkit, with Henry Korman. Bantam Books. 1989.

Desktop Publishing, with Carlene Schnabel. Ballantine Books. 1987.

How to Write a Computer Manual. Benjamin/Cummings. 1984.

Put That in Writing. Viking Press and Penguin Books. 1984.

The Instant Expert's Guide to BASIC on the IBM PC. Dell. 1984.

The Definitive Word Processing Book, with Linda Urban. Viking Press and Penguin Books. 1984.

How to Find Work. New American Library. 1982.

Thirty Days to More Powerful Writing. Fawcett Books and Ballantine Books. 1981. Reprinted for Crown Books. 1982.

Three by Ben Jonson: Volpone, The Alchemist, and Mercury Vindicated from the Alkemists at Court, (Editor) New American Library. 1980.

Classic Scenes, edited and translated. New American Library. 1979.

The Best Thing on TV: Commercials. Viking Press, Penguin Books, Quality Paperback Club. 1978.

Video Visions: A Medium Discovers Itself. New American Library. 1977.

Life Show Anthology: 9 Plays from the Sixties, co-edited with John Lahr. Bantam Books. 1973.

Life Show: How to See Theater in Life and Life in Theater, with John Lahr. Viking Press and Penguin Books. 1973. Reissued by Limelight Editions, 1990.

On Finnegans Wake (pamphlet). Grove Press. 1972.

Critics on Robert Lowell (editor). University of Miami Press. 1972. U.K. edition: Allen and Unwin.

Made in the USA
Monee, IL
18 November 2019

16973142R00105